# The Architecture of Frank Furness

# The Architecture of Frank Furness

by James F. O'Gorman

**Catalogue of Selected Buildings**
by George E. Thomas
and James F. O'Gorman

**Checklist of the Architecture
and Projects of Frank Furness**
by George E. Thomas
and Hyman Myers

**Addendum to the Checklist**
by George E. Thomas, Hyman Myers,
and Jeffrey A. Cohen

Special Photography
by Cervin Robinson

**Philadelphia Museum of Art**

Published on the occasion
of the exhibition
at the Philadelphia Museum of Art
April 5 to May 27, 1973

Cover:
Chapel, Mount Sinai Cemetery
Exterior detail from southwest

Frontispiece:
Frank Furness, 1906
Courtesy George Wood Furness

The authors dedicate their work to
William M. Campbell
John F. Harbeson
David M. Robb and
Theo B. White
who first taught them to see
Philadelphia's Victorian Architecture

Copyright 1973 by the Philadelphia Museum of Art
Additional copyright 1987 by the Philadelphia Museum of Art
Box 7646, Philadelphia, Pa. 19101

Printed in the United States of America
by The Falcon Press, Philadelphia

Designed by Eugene Feldman

**Library of Congress Cataloging-in-Publication Data**

O'Gorman, James F.
    The architecture of Frank Furness.
    Originally published on the occasion of the exhibition at the Philadelphia
Museum of Art, Apr. 5–May 27, 1973.
    Contents: Catalogue of selected buildings / by George E. Thomas and
James F. O'Gorman—Checklist of the architecture and projects of Frank
Furness / by George E. Thomas and Hyman Myers—Addendum to the
checklist / by George E. Thomas, Hyman Myers, and Jeffrey A. Cohen—[etc.]
    1. Furness, Frank, 1839–1912—Exhibitions.   2. Architecture, Modern—
19th century—United States—Exhibitions.   3. Architecture, Modern—20th
century—United States—Exhibitions.   4. Architecture—United States—
Exhibitions.
I. Philadelphia Museum of Art.   II. Title.
NA737.F85A4     1987     720'.92'4     87–11339
ISBN 0-87633-015-4 (Phila. Museum of Art: pbk)
ISBN 0-8122-7957-3 (Univ. of Pa. Press: cloth)

Distributed in cloth by
University of Pennsylvania Press
Blockley Hall, 418 Service Drive
Philadelphia, Pa. 19104

**Checklist of the Architecture and Projects of Frank Furness**
by George E. Thomas and Hyman Myers

**Addendum to the Checklist**
by George E. Thomas, Hyman Myers,
and Jeffrey A. Cohen

**Key to Abbreviated References**

| | |
|---|---|
| *AABN* | *American Architect and Building News* |
| *HABS* | *Historic American Building Survey* |
| *JSAH* | *Journal of the Society of Architectural Historians* |
| Massey 1 | James C. Massey, "Frank Furness in the 1870's," *Charette,* 43. January 1963, pp. 13–16. |
| Massey 2 | James C. Massey, "Frank Furness in the 1880's," *Charette,* 43. October 1963, pp. 25–29. |
| Massey 3 | James C. Massey, "Frank Furness: The Declining Years," *Charette,* 46, February 1966, pp. 9–13. |
| *PI* | *Philadelphia Inquirer* |
| *PRERBG* | *Philadelphia Real Estate Record and Builders' Guide* |
| Tatum | George B. Tatum, *Penn's Great Town*, Philadelphia, 1961. |

# Foreword

Among historians of American architecture the name of Frank Furness was remembered long after his death in 1912 because of the appreciative observations made by Louis Sullivan in his *Autobiography of an Idea*. In Philadelphia the name was also remembered—it was after all the name of a family that had contributed significantly to the city's intellectual life, the architect's father having been a Unitarian divine and his brother, a noted Shakespearean scholar —and his buildings were at least tolerated, albeit more often than not with condescension. The major works that he created to fulfill the spiritual and cultural needs of the city—the Pennsylvania Academy of the Fine Arts, the Library of the University of Pennsylvania, the various churches, most notably that created for his father's parish—have survived, although not always unharmed; but many of the structures built to answer the commercial demands of an expanding city have over the years been torn down.

In fact, virtually half of his work no longer exists, and a considerable part of that still standing has been gravely marred. Repeatedly, improvements made in the interests of "good taste" have sadly undermined the force of the Furness concept. Feeling great concern that these fine buildings should suffer such a fate and believing that a more widespread appreciation of a distinguished achievement is the best guarantee of its salvation in the future, the Philadelphia Museum of Art has created, as one of its major exhibitions of the 1972–1973 season, a retrospective consideration of the architecture of Frank Furness. This volume is published on that occasion.

The material presented here is the work of a group of scholars. James O'Gorman's interest in Frank Furness developed during his years of teaching at the University of Pennsylvania. The vitality with which he has nurtured understanding of America's nineteenth-century architecture—often still a source of humor or horror—is effectively evident in the essay of this book. The catalogue is the result of the collaboration of Professor O'Gorman and one of his former students, who is today the leading authority on Philadelphia's nineteenth-century architecture. This scholar, George Thomas, has pursued his researches with energy, imagination, and an admirable method. Rather than depend upon the all-too-vague traditions of family suppositions and the city's word-of-mouth, he has methodically read Philadelphia's newspapers from 1865 onwards, seeking the information contained in the building permits which were then published, afterwards checking the addresses in the annual city directories to be sure that the buildings had in fact been completed. Philadelphia in the years following the Centennial was justly proud of its rapid growth; thus newspapers of the day recognized, fortunately for today's scholars, that publication of stories on the latest architectural accomplishments found a ready audience. A wealth of little-known material is still available for the architectural historian; this publication is one of the first works to reflect this new method of searching it out. The checklist is the joint effort of Mr. Thomas and Philadelphia architect Hyman Myers, who developed a deep interest in Frank Furness while pursuing his studies in Furness's University Library. His constant enthusiasm and knowledgeable criticism, and that of photographer Cervin Robinson, himself an architectural historian, contributed to maintaining the high standards of scholarship throughout this book.

Documentary evidence is essential for the scholar, but stylistic analysis remains of prime importance. On the basis of the individuality of Furness's style, such an analysis may occasionally aid in establishing the extent of his participation in the buildings designed by the various firms in which he was involved. As an example—which also points up how surprisingly difficult it can be to reach firm conclusions on even such a relatively recent period—scholars have never been able to establish which Philadelphia house inspired Louis Sullivan's words: "On the west side of South Broad Street a residence, almost completed, caught his eye like a flower by the roadside. . . . Here was something fresh and fair to him, a human note, as though someone were talking." His admiration for this house, which he learned was by Furness and Hewitt, led him to go to Furness and demand acceptance as an apprentice. He was accepted, but because of the city's sudden financial panic in the autumn of 1873, the relationship was short-lived. The experience remained, however, a vivid one as Sullivan's own distinguished career developed in Chicago. It is no surprise that establishing the identity of the house is a challenge that has long teased scholars.

Only with the research for this publication have Messrs. Thomas and Myers discovered that the admired house was one closely associated with the history of the Philadelphia Museum of Art. Previously, careful study of photographs of the fashionable houses lining Broad Street had proved futile, for none presented a façade displaying the Furness individuality. However, when these scholars began to study views of the sides and backs of various major houses they spotted characteristic brickwork and details confirming that the now-destroyed 510 South Broad Street was in fact the house which had so stirred Louis Sullivan. This was a house built for one of the Museum's earliest major donors, the voracious collector Mrs. Bloomfield Moore. Later scholars could not identify the house as a Furness work because its next owner but one, the distinguished lawyer and connoisseur, John G. Johnson, had had the street façade redesigned shortly after he purchased the house, to reflect a more recent trend in architectural taste, the French Gothic style. One can hardly help but speculate about the aura of a house that nurtured two such distinguished collectors!

The Philadelphia Museum of Art has long had an even closer association with a work created by the Furness office, namely the so-called Sanctuary attached to the Museum-administered Samuel S. Fleisher Art Memorial at Seventh and Catharine Streets. In fact, a church originally, it was built in 1886 by Furness, Evans and Company for the Church of the Evangelists and designed, according to Mr. Thomas, by Louis C. Baker and E. James Dallett. It is a forceful example of the Furness tradition, which happily crops up again and again throughout the greater Philadelphia area.

Frank Furness's career spanned what may well be considered the most creative period in the history of Philadelphia. The years following the Centennial were indeed distinguished ones, and the city was proud, understandably secure in its sense of accomplishment. One of the nation's largest parks, on the shores of the Schuylkill River, had gained worldwide attention because of the great international exposition that had been spread across its slopes.

The creation of the Fairmount Park Art Association, dedicated to the sculptural adornment of these park lands and the city's streets, nurtured a sense of responsibility that would come to have a significant impact upon Philadelphia's future urban development. The city had one of the finest art schools in America in the Pennsylvania Academy of the Fine Arts and the nation's first Zoological Society, and its University was entering into a period of great expansion.

Remarkable individuals were adding to the luster of the city's aesthetic existence. Thomas Eakins was painting some of the finest pictures ever created by an American artist. George Roberts had carved those few marbles which can only make posterity regret that he chose to do so little. Alexander Milne Calder was absorbed in producing hundreds of figures to decorate Philadelphia's vast new City Hall, a municipal building without equal in the nation. Numerous architects were answering the needs of a growing city. It is, therefore, even more impressive that in a period of such distinguished accomplishment, Frank Furness remained an outstanding figure; his buildings gave character to a city widely admired for its style.

Evan H. Turner
Director

## Acknowledgments

An undertaking as complex as this publication and exhibition depends upon the assistance and good will of a great many individuals. The owners and tenants of the various buildings were most generous in permitting repeated inspection and photography of their premises, and the success of this effort is due in large measure to their patience and cooperation. Their interest in this project is reflected in the appearance of their buildings in the catalogue. Many of these are privately owned, and their inclusion here and in the exhibition does not indicate that they are open to the public.

The authors and the Philadelphia Museum of Art express their gratitude to the following individuals and institutions: Harrison Albrecht; Mrs. E. Page Allinson; Archives and Fine Arts Library, University of Pennsylvania; Thomas N. Armstrong, 3rd; Baltimore and Ohio Railroad Company; Robert Barfield; Penelope Batchelor; Ken Carroll; Percy Clark; Congregation Rodeph Shalom; F. James Dallett; James L. Dillon and Co., Inc.; Einstein Medical Center; Edward Eisen; First Troop, Philadelphia City Cavalry; First Unitarian Church; Free Library of Philadelphia; Edward Gray; Mr. and Mrs. John R. Griffith, III; Mr. and Mrs. Alfred W. Hesse, Jr.; Historical Society of Pennsylvania; Historic American Building Survey; Independence Hall National Park; Benjamin Jacobson; Library Company of Philadelphia; Library of Congress; S. Miller; Lois Morasco; Alan Morrison; Peter Parker; Penn-Central Company; The Pennsylvania Academy of the Fine Arts; Philadelphia Saving Fund Society; Philadelphia Zoological Society; Mr. and Mrs. Alexander Phillips; The Provident Mutual Life Insurance Company; Reading Railroad Company; Seamen's Church Institute; Raymond V. Shepherd, Jr.; Mrs. Elizabeth Snodgrass; Dr. George B. Tatum; Rabbi Richard Steinbrink; Robert Stubbs; Thomas Jefferson University; Rabbi David H. Wice; Williamson Free School; the owners of the William Winsor house; and Richard Saul Wurman.

The interest and encouragement and the contributions of the following are gratefully acknowledged: The American Philosophical Society awarded a grant to Hyman Myers for research on the architecture of Frank Furness. William M. Campbell gave access to his research on Furness. His information about Furness's University Library is of great importance, and his contact with the surviving members of Furness's firm was communicated freely. George Eisenman of James L. Dillon and Co., Inc., located old photographs from his firm's files and did most of the copy work on a crash basis. Herbert Levy, architect for the Einstein Medical Center, located drawings, blueprints, and building fragments. Hugh McCauley and Marianna M. Thomas produced many drawings, which provide insight into the architect's work. David A. Stupplebeen made his drawings and valuable research on the University Library available for this project. Edward Teitelman pointed out a number of sources and added to our information.

Above all, the members of the architect's family, Edward Duer, Horace H. Jayne, Timothy Jayne, Charles C. Savage, and George Wood Furness gave freely of their time. Mr. Furness, in particular, opened to us family documents, scrapbooks, and materials without which our understanding of Frank Furness would have been far less complete and less interesting.

## Preface

David M. Robb and Theo B. White first suggested that I write about Frank Furness. James C. Massey long ago introduced me to the architect's work. Whatever virtues the essay possesses are heavily dependent upon the grass-roots research of George E. Thomas and Hyman Myers, the drawings of Marianna M. Thomas and Hugh McCauley, the criticism of Cervin Robinson, and the stimulating late-night sessions during which we all talked at once. Our collaboration has been a model of cooperative scholarship. Margaret Floyd, Michael Eramo, Susan Fondiler, John Herzan, Mary Holden, Kathleen Laughlin, William Lebovich, Robert McKay, Michele Noble, Brian Pfeiffer, Ned Reynolds, and Stephen Roper—members of my seminar on the atelier of Richard Morris Hunt, given at Boston University in Fall 1972—each contributed insights into Furness's context. Other, more specific assistance is acknowledged in the notes.

I want to thank the Philadelphia Museum of Art for the opportunity to discuss Furness's career, particularly Evan H. Turner who from the beginning enthusiastically backed the idea of an exhibition. Mary Lea Bandy and George H. Marcus gave needed editorial direction; Eugene Feldman conceived the effective layout.

Finally, I am fundamentally indebted to the generosity and encouragement of three members of the architect's family: Timothy Jayne, Charles C. Savage, and especially, George Wood Furness. Without their active support there would have been no exhibition and no publication.

J.F.O'G.

Bay View, Cape Ann, Massachusetts
January 1973

# The Architecture of Frank Furness

James F. O'Gorman

1 Philadelphia: Arch Street Methodist Church, 1868, by Addison Hutton; Masonic Temple, 1867–73, by James Windrim; City Hall, begun 1871, by John McArthur, Jr. Photograph by Cervin Robinson

## Introduction

Victorian Philadelphia was a hierarchical cluster of towers (fig. 1). Until the recent mushrooming of downtown, glass-walled superblocks, the central shaft of City Hall dominated a pattern of urban districts grouped around subsidiary towers. This picturesque cityscape was created out of new economic and social forces by the architects who began to work in the years following the Civil War. Frank Furness was one of them. They found Philadelphia a horizontal, Georgian-based town in which William Penn's gridiron rose three to five brick stories above the pavement, punctuated here and there with a Neoclassical bank, a Romanesque church, or a pilastered factory. They left it a city of vertical sprouts ready, through further economic and technological developments, to grow into the present city of skyscrapers. In the Victorian city the real or wishful status of every institution in contemporary society could be indicated by the location of its building, the richness of the building's surface and silhouette, and the height and number of its towers. The towers were the essential features of the cityscape. They served as Gothic, Roman, or Italic exclamation points within the typography of the urban story.

In 1871 John McArthur, Jr., began the government center at Broad and Market streets, in the heart of the gridiron, where Latrobe's waterworks had once stood in a public garden. City Hall eventually thrust Billy Penn 548 feet into the air, placing him as the city's guiding historical spirit atop a tower that still proclaims the building as the central axis of power between the Delaware and Schuylkill rivers. Around this urban axis Frank Furness and other postwar architects grouped a series of smaller buildings that echoed its vertical emphasis, their towers of lesser status pinning down supporting institutions: finance, transportation, commerce, culture, religion, and the home. Furness designed for all these institutions and more, mostly within his native city, its suburbs, or along the lines of communication radiating outward from the city. His work in particular nestled around the vertical axis of City Hall, and should be understood in its urban role, as part of the growing concentric fabric of a post–Civil War American city.

Just west of City Hall Furness erected the Pennsylvania Railroad's Broad Street Station, its lower but animated silhouette proclaiming railroading the powerful partner of government in the Gilded Age (cat. 33). Just to the south rose the West End Trust to group banking with railroading and government in the center of post–Civil War life (cat. 39). To the north, on Broad, stands the established and conservative Pennsylvania Academy of the Fine Arts, rich in polychromy but reserved in its traditional low tripartite front (cat. 3). Eastward rose new banking houses for the Guarantee (cat. 6), the Provident (cat. 14), and other institutions in the old financial district, their aggressive façades reflecting the new world of business. North, south, and west of City Hall in a concentric circle of greater radius lay the new domestic areas, focused upon asymmetrically spired ecclesiastical structures such as Rodef Shalom (cat. 2), Holy Apostles (cat. 1), or the First Unitarian (cat. 24), the houses civilly aligned in rows but vying with one another in surface elaboration according to the wealth and aspiration of the owners (cat. 9 and 37). Farther to the west, on the banks of the Schuylkill, stations for the B & O (cat. 26) and the Pennsy sounded diminished reverberations of Broad Street Station; and beyond, in West Philadelphia, the Library of the University of Pennsylvania rose tower-and-chimney above the new academic center as its cultural and architectural standard (cat. 29). Still farther, along the outlying railroad tracks of the Pennsy and the Reading, were Furness-designed depots (cat. 19) that provided sheltered focal points of arrival and departure for residents of suburban homes set into the sprawling landscape of Media, Fox Chase (cat. 18), Haverford (cat. 20), and so on. Finally, Samuel Shipley's water tower at "Winden" in West Chester carried the vertical theme to its faintest echo in exurbia (cat. 22-1).

As much as anyone Furness gave shape to Victorian Philadelphia. His were among the most boisterous and challenging buildings in an age and city noted for aggressive architecture. We have inherited the nineteenth-century city of towers, but in the last twenty-five years commercial rivalry and cultural indifference have altered its meaning and destroyed many of the individual buildings of Furness and his contemporaries. In the following essay, primarily devoted to the selection of forty buildings featured in the accompanying exhibition, we shall see some of what Philadelphia has lost of Furness's work, and some of what survives.

The essay is exploratory. It assumes that Furness's personality and training are relevant factors in a preliminary understanding of his work. It also assumes that work to be extraordinary but explicable within the general architectural context of Furness's own time.

## 1. Furness and His Family (1839–67)

On the evening of November 9, 1870, the Reverend William Henry Furness delivered in Philadelphia the closing address to the fourth annual convention of the American Institute of Architects.[1] It was as characteristic of the architectural profession in the mid-nineteenth century to have a man of the cloth give such a speech as it would be of the present A.I.A. to have a scientist address its convention, but Dr. Furness gave no pious homily on ecclesiology. After protesting his lack of knowledge about the subject, he urged the assembled architects to take professional pride in architecture as a fine art allied with nature and entreated them to avoid the easy conformity that outsiders would impose upon them. He assured them that they would receive much adverse comment from the public, especially if they tried to break out of the mold. The unfamiliar would be rejected out of hand, he said.

> With all our freedom, we do not tolerate oddness. We insist, in this country, upon everything's being cut to one pattern. Only think what a long day of it, one particular style of building (the Quaker style—marble steps and wooden shutters) has had here in Philadelphia. . . . It is an adventurous thing . . . to set before us anything of which we cannot at once tell what to think. We resent it . . . and take satisfaction—the law of taste—into our own hands, and condemn it.

Despite this warning Dr. Furness closed with a plea that his listeners create the "new orders of architecture," which "universal liberty . . . a vital principle" demanded of them in the same degree that "we require new styles of building fitted to" the use of iron.

For an outsider Dr. Furness proved himself well read in the subject, familiar at least with the most important architectural theoreticians of the time: Pugin, Ruskin, perhaps Viollet-le-Duc. And his speech must have filled his listeners with the professional pride he asked of them, for he said that he did not "know whether in any department, whether even in literature, with Shakespeare at its head, there has been a more imposing display of human genius than in architecture."

1. Don Gifford, ed., *The Literature of Architecture,* New York, 1966, pp. 390 ff.

2. Furness was elected to the A.I.A. on March 19, 1866; by October 1873 his membership had lapsed. See the *Proceedings of the Sixteenth Annual Convention of the American Institute of Architects*, Newport, 1883, p. 73. He was among the founders of the Philadelphia Chapter in 1869.

3. H. H. F. Jayne, ed., *The Letters of Horace Howard Furness*, 2 vols., Boston and New York, 1922, I, pp. xvi ff., contains a discussion of the family. Additional material will be found in any good biographical dictionary, such as the *Biographical Dictionary of America* or the *Dictionary of American Biography*.
Furness was a descendant of Jacob Hurd, famed eighteenth-century Boston silversmith (1702-58), via Jacob's daughter Anne, who married John Furnass (*sic*). They had four children, one of whom was John Mason Furnass (1763-1804), the Boston portrait painter. The Philadelphia Furnesses, however, descend from John and Anne's youngest child, William. See Hollis French, *Jacob Hurd and His Sons*, Cambridge, Mass., 1939. I am indebted to Kathryn C. Buhler and George Wood Furness, Frank Furness's grandson, for pointing out these connections.

4. A. A. Gilchrist, *William Strickland*, Philadelphia, 1950, pp. 77-78.

5. H[orace] H[oward] F[urness], *Records of a Lifelong Friendship*, Boston, 1910. This contains the Furness-Emerson correspondence.

6. Among the "major American gift books," *The Diadem . . . a Present for All Seasons* contained a treasury of the visual and verbal arts, including works by Emerson, John Sartain, Emanuel Leutze, Edmund Landseer, and others. It was published in 1845, 1846, and 1847 by Carey and Hart in Philadelphia, and should not be confused with *The Diadem; A Souvenir for the Drawing Room and Parlor, and Gift Book for all Seasons*, edited by Emily Percival and published in Boston and New York in 1853. See Ralph Thompson, *American Literary Annuals and Gift Books 1825-1865*, New York, 1936, pp. 78-81, 118, 125.

7. *Records*, p. 34.

8. *Records*, p. 86. On May 27, 1890, James Martineau wrote to Dr. Furness that "it is delightful to hear how blest you are in your sons & daughters [*sic*]." *Translations of the Colonial Society of Massachusetts*, VIII, 1902-4, pp. 134 ff.

This statement is particularly noteworthy because in 1870 one of Dr. Furness's surviving sons had recently embarked on a lifetime of editing Shakespeare's works, and the second, who we must assume heard this address,[2] had as recently begun a career in architecture—a career that was to answer the pastor's plea for an end to the "Quaker style." The relationship of this gifted father to equally talented children is basic to an understanding of Frank Furness and his work. The architect must be introduced as a member of Dr. Furness's remarkable family.

Frank grew up in a cultured, middle-class domestic atmosphere that was Unitarian and abolitionist, intellectual and artistic. The strong sense of rectitude, of achievement, of determination, of creative imagination that marked the Furness family as a whole, characterized Frank in particular. Perhaps his position as the youngest of four children in a closely knit, highly accomplished family made him try harder.

When Frank was born on November 12, 1839, the family lived at 1426 Pine Street, one of those ubiquitous Philadelphia "Quaker style" brick town houses mentioned by Dr. Furness to the A.I.A.; but the Furnesses were not native Philadelphians. William Henry Furness (1802-1896) was a Bostonian educated at Harvard College (1820) and Harvard Divinity School (1823).[3] In 1825 he moved to Philadelphia to become pastor of the First Congregational Unitarian Church, a flock established in 1796 by the famed scientist Joseph Priestley, but without spiritual leadership for a quarter of a century. Providing the congregation in 1828 with a new church at Tenth and Locust—an austere Pennsylvania marble box with Greek Doric portico designed by William Strickland[4]— William Henry Furness settled into a long and distinguished pastorate. He became pastor emeritus in 1875, and within a decade Frank would replace Strickland's building with the present First Unitarian Church at Chestnut and Van Pelt.

William Henry Furness's interests were not confined to his church. He turned out lecture after lecture, volume after volume on the New Testament; he preached—at times to the chagrin of his congregation and the peril of his own and his family's well-being—the abolition of slavery; and, practicing what he preached, turned his cellar into a way station on the underground railroad and opened his parlor to other antislavers such as William Ellery Channing, William Lloyd Garrison, and Wendell Phillips. Abolition was probably the chief topic of conversation in the Furness house during the 1840s and 1850s, Frank's formative years. But not even that crusade absorbed all of Dr. Furness's energies. His dedication to English and German literature and his lifelong friendship with Ralph Waldo Emerson[5] involved him with belles-lettres and the brief editing of *The Diadem* in the mid-forties.[6] He was also a draftsman of some talent. In short, William Henry Furness embraced the fine and practical arts, literature, religion, scholarship, and civil rights. Emerson recognized these many facets when he wrote to Furness in 1844 that he was "glad so many Muses sacred & more sacred contend for you. . . ."[7] None of these many interests was unknown to his children; in fact, each of them seems to have selected one and made it his own. Dr. Furness wrote to Emerson in 1852 that "one has great satisfaction in living in one's children."[8]

There were four: William Henry junior (1828-1867); Annis Lee ("Nan" or "Annie"; 1830-1908); Horace Howard (1833-1912); and Frank. Annie, who married Dr. Caspar Wistar in 1854, followed her father's interest in German

Plate 1 Church of the Holy Apostles. Exterior detail from west

literature, gaining some reputation as a translator. The eldest son picked up his father's undeveloped talent for graphic art, becoming a portrait draftsman of some renown in his own time if not in ours. From the mid-1840s on William junior worked in Philadelphia and Boston and studied in Europe at Munich and Düsseldorf. A regular exhibitor in Boston, Philadelphia, and New York, he was in the midst of a promising career when he died in Cambridge, Massachusetts, at thirty-nine, just at the outset of Frank's own professional life.[9] The eldest son must have had a significant influence upon the youngest, reinforcing Dr. Furness's attraction to drawing, for in 1859 Frank listed himself with William in *McElroy's Philadelphia City Directory* as an "artist." Frank's own able draftsmanship sprang from that of his father, began to develop under William's eye, and reached its maturity in the atelier of Richard Morris Hunt.

William's death removed him from Frank's life relatively early, but the architect's career paralleled in time that of the other son. Horace was a scholar who, unlike his brothers, followed his father to Harvard (class of '54) and after two years of travel in Europe, studied law and was admitted to the Philadelphia bar in 1859. Deafness kept him from active duty in the Civil War, just as ill health prevented William from any participation in the conflict, but the family's abolitionist sentiment led Horace into service with the Sanitary Commission under Frederick Law Olmsted. After the war Horace turned to his lifework, the *New Variorum Shakespeare* (the first volume appeared in 1871), and a professorship at the University of Pennsylvania, where he was later to head the building committee for the library designed by his brother. Sharing his work on the Bard were both Horace's wife, Helen Kate Rogers, who compiled a *Concordance* to the poetry, and his son, Horace Howard junior, who continued the *Variorum*.[10]

Frank Furness, then, grew up in a family that was as involved as it was reflective, as intellectual as it was artistic, and totally motivated by the spirit of Dr. Furness. Writing in the year of William's death, and in characteristic Victorian terms, Henry T. Tuckerman described this domestic ambience and what he thought to have been its consequences. Although it refers to the eldest son, it applies to the youngest as well:

> Educated in an atmosphere of truth, the culture and character of his father early impressed him with high and holy aims; for the genuine, the aspiring, and the ideal his sympathies were soon enlisted; a singular refinement of nature prepared him to seek in art no meretricious or casual end, but the realization of principles, the latent truth of nature.[11]

The last part of this quotation has a direct bearing upon Frank's work, especially in the realm of decoration.

Frank's own schooling ended early. We assume that he chose to emulate his oldest brother's artistic career rather than compete in scholarship with other family members. He did not go to Harvard (although Emerson supposed he would[12]) and, in the absence of documentation to the contrary, it is assumed that he never got to Europe. In his teens he was learning draftsmanship in the Philadelphia office of John Fraser, who was to be briefly his partner after the war—and then he encountered Richard Morris Hunt.

His entry into the Hunt atelier in New York resulted from a network of typical family relationships.[13] As Frank later recalled, Hunt, fresh from Europe, had come to visit William, whom he had known in Paris; he began to talk of architecture, and captivated the youngest Furness with his brilliant draftsmanship.

9. George C. Groce and David H. Wallace, *The New-York Historical Society's Dictionary of Artists in America*, New Haven, 1957, p. 246. Timothy Jayne of Oxford, Pa., has some manuscript material.

10. Jayne, *Letters*, passim.

11. Henry T. Tuckerman, *Book of the Artists*, New York, 1867, p. 481.

12. *Records*, p. 95.

13. Our knowledge of Furness's stay in Hunt's atelier comes from a memoir of the period by Furness. It exists in two typescripts: one of six pages, single spaced, 8 by 12 inches; the other of twenty-eight pages, triple spaced, 8½ by 11 inches. It is among the architect's papers now in the possession of George Wood Furness. The typed texts are identical, but the second version contains revisions in Furness's angular handwriting. Most of the statements by Furness concerning the atelier quoted below come from the revised memoir. Small sections of the unrevised version were published by Alan Burnham in "The New York Architecture of Richard Morris Hunt," *JSAH*, XI, May 1952, p. 11. The fact that the unrevised memoir appears in the Hunt Papers compiled by Mrs. Hunt suggests that the memoir might have been written for her, and later revised. It was certainly originally written after Hunt's death in 1895.

It was just about this time that two of Horace's friends from Harvard, Charles Dexter Gambrill (1834–1880) and Henry Van Brunt (1832–1903), together with George B. Post (1837–1913), prevailed upon Hunt to offer instruction in architecture in New York where he had just opened his office and designed the Studio Building. There was no professional school of architecture in the United States at the time; Hunt's atelier was the birthplace of professional architectural education in this country.

Furness entered the atelier in the spring of 1859,[14] and remained until after the outbreak of war in the spring of 1861. He spent the summer of 1860 at Newport where Hunt was beginning to design Stick Style buildings, such as the Griswold House, that were to be so influential in Furness's own later domestic architecture. Hostilities interrupted his plans to pursue his training in Europe for, as he much later so laconically wrote, "instead of going to Paris, I went to Virginia, serving in the army for the next four [he meant three] years." A lifelong lover of horses, Furness joined the Union cavalry in October 1861, and by the time of his discharge in October 1864 had risen to the rank of Captain, Company F, 6th Pennsylvanian (fig. 2). He might have been one of the many cavalry officers sketched in Virginia by a young artist-correspondent named Winslow Homer. With those abolitionist conversations of the 1850s ringing in his ears (their antiwar sentiment presumably forgotten), Furness served his cause with bravery. Although he refused recognition for his efforts at the time, in 1899 he petitioned for and received the Congressional Medal of Honor for his actions at Trevilian Station, Virginia, on June 12, 1864, when, to quote his citation, he "voluntarily carried a box of ammunition across an open space swept by the enemy's fire to the relief of an outpost whose ammunition had become almost exhausted, but which was thus enabled to hold its important position."[15] Frank Furness is the only American architect of note to have received his country's highest military award.

Furness returned to New York following his discharge late in 1864 to assume a position of responsibility, according to his own account, in Hunt's office.[16] He probably worked for Hunt during 1865, but by 1866 he was back in Philadelphia to marry Fannie Fassitt and begin his architectural career. They lived with his father until the early 1870s, when, Frank's career well launched with the commission for the Pennsylvania Academy of the Fine Arts, they moved into their own house at 711 Locust Street—a "Quaker style" rowhouse outside, but as wild as the west within.[17]

## 2. England and France

Until the last years of the nineteenth century, the architecture of the United States was shaped mainly by the influence of English and French taste. The architecture of the Early Republic resulted largely from the confluence of these two imported traditions. In the work of Jefferson or Latrobe the inspiration of Paris and London, of Ledoux and Soane, mingled in about equal parts; while McIntire and Bulfinch were more complete Anglophiles; and Ramée and Godefroy, like L'Enfant, were French immigrants.

At the time of the Civil War and after, these same two fonts still provided the main inspiration for American architects—with a certain, at present ill-defined, admixture of German ideas as well.[18] But the theory and practice of architecture had changed radically in the intervening half-century. International Neoclassicism had given way before a host of new ideas. Since it is impossible

2 Frank Furness as a cavalry officer, 1860s. Courtesy George Wood Furness

14. The memoir is not specific, but George Wood Furness possesses a letter written by Hunt to Dr. Furness accepting Frank as his student. It is dated April 1, 1859.

15. *The Medal of Honor of the United States Army,* Washington, D.C., 1948, p. 161. The fact that he earlier refused brevets comes from an endorsement of Furness's petition by Maj. General W. Merritt dated August 12, 1899, in George Wood Furness's possession.

16. See note 55.

17. Furness had four children: Radclyffe, Theodore Fassitt, James Wilson, and Annie.

18. "The three influences, English, French, and German, to which we owe our architecture, are pretty clearly shown [in the architectural exhibition at the Centennial in Philadelphia]. . . .The English . . . predominates in the Boston work, and is very prominent in . . . New York. The French . . . is stronger in the New York section than elsewhere, though it leaves some trace [in] Boston and other Eastern work. The German [is marked] in the Western work." *AABN,* I, June 24, 1876, p. 203.

3 John Ruskin. "Pierced Ornaments from Lisieux, Bayeux, Verona, and Padua" (from *The Seven Lamps of Architecture*, 1849, Pl. VII)

4 G. E. Street. "Examples of Italian Brickwork from Verona, Milan, Brescia, Monza, and S. Fermo Maggiore" (from *Brick and Marble in the Middle Ages*, 1855, Pl. 34)

19. Kenneth Clark, *The Gothic Revival*, 2d ed., London, 1962.

20. The story is of course more complicated than this summation suggests. The exact relationship between the book and the building is still a matter of dispute, as is Ruskin's precise relationship to High Victorian Gothic. Ruskin himself certainly envisioned something else, but his and Butterfield's work merged in the minds of others. For a recent discussion of these problems, see George Hersey, *High Victorian Gothic*, Baltimore, 1972, pp. 183 ff.

here to examine all aspects of mid-century architecture and theory in London and Paris, English High Victorian Gothic will be briefly considered as a reflection of the ideas of John Ruskin (1819–1900) and the designs of William Butterfield (1814–1900), while the architecture of Second Empire France will be represented by the work of Henri Labrouste (1801–1875), the teaching of the École des Beaux-Arts, and the theory of Eugène-Emmanuel Viollet-le-Duc (1814–1879). The most provocative stimulants for the postwar American architect will be found in these sources. It depended upon his training and associations which font he tapped more often, although his position permitted him to combine English and French precedents.

High Victorian Gothic architecture was born in England in 1849 as the third phase of the Gothic Revival that began as a literary affectation with Horace Walpole and others in the eighteenth century, and grew into a set of religious and nationalistic associations under A. W. N. Pugin in the 1830s and 1840s.[19] This third phase of the Revival, sometimes called the "polychrome picturesque" phase, was to last in its home country through the 1870s, and in America well beyond. In 1849 Ruskin published his *Seven Lamps of Architecture*, which, with his *Stones of Venice* of 1851–53 (and the publications of the Ecclesiological Society), established the theoretical foundation of the period, just as William Butterfield's design for the church of All Saints', Margaret Street, also begun in 1849 although not dedicated until 1859, became its first important exemplar. The book and the building form the dual platform upon which High Victorian Gothic architecture was built.[20]

First, the book. Again we must extract some key points from the verbal deluge that was Ruskin's prose style. It can be said that he influenced mid nineteenth-century architecture in at least three ways: 1) by advocating the medieval architecture of northern Italy as the style best adapted to nineteenth-century needs, 2) by expounding an esthetic theory that was moralistic and naturalistic, and 3) by perceiving and discussing buildings as if they were conglomerations of heterogeneous surface details. The first, about which we hear the most, was certainly of greater importance in England than in America.

Ruskin hated classical and Renaissance building. For him the polychromatic richness of Italian medieval architecture, specifically the Gothic of Florence, Verona, and Venice, epitomized the art of architecture. Buildings like the Doge's Palace in Venice perfectly fitted the criteria of criticism outlined in the *Seven Lamps,* where architecture is illuminated beneath the torches of Sacrifice, Truth, Power, Beauty, Life, Memory, and Obedience—their titles alone dramatizing the gulf between nineteenth-century architectural poetry and the prose of our own day. "Truth" reiterates Pugin's moral stand: there is to be no sham, no imitation of one material by another or one technique by another. Polychromy was to result from the direct expression of parti-colored materials. "Life" affirmed that a building should express the fullness of human experience, embrace boldness and irregularity, and scorn refinement, although the Lamp of Power recommended, with only slight contradiction, simple massing. "Obedience" justified the use of historical precedent despite the Lamp of Memory, which saw the history of a civilization written in its buildings. But it is the two remaining Lamps—of Sacrifice and of Beauty—that contain the kernel of Ruskin's thought.

The Lamp of Sacrifice lays down the law that ornament distinguishes "architecture" from mere building. In fact, architecture for Ruskin is ornament, *period*—the addition to the structural vehicle of useless detail to produce beauty. This already limiting view is restricted further by Ruskin's concept of beauty which, we discover in the light of this Lamp, is alone to be found in the exact imitation of natural forms. Ruskin shared this esthetic position with the painters of the Pre-Raphaelite Brotherhood (founded in 1848) and put it into practice in his contributions to Deane and Woodward's University Museum in Oxford (1855), where the window surrounds are enriched with carved stone flora and fauna, some designed by members of the Brotherhood at Ruskin's request. The Oxford Museum is a natural history museum, and both amateur and professional interest in the natural sciences—particularly botany, geology, and zoology—was a constituent aspect of nineteenth-century English culture. The celebration of nature through the minute copying of natural forms as architectural ornament—for which there was medieval precedent in such works as the Chapter House at Southwell—became after mid-century a key element of architectural style, reaffirmed by art and science alike. And it fit perfectly into the philosophical and artistic worship of nature that characterizes nineteenth-century American culture from Thomas Jefferson to Thomas Cole to Henry David Thoreau, and was encapsulated in A. B. Durand's *Kindred Spirits* of 1849 (New York Public Library) in which a painter and a poet are depicted deep in a forest. In this scientific and esthetic focus upon nature, Ruskin struck his most responsive chord in the United States. Progressive thinkers felt that this love of nature would develop here, in the "garden of the world," far beyond what it had done in Europe.[21] As the son of a friend and correspondent of Ralph Waldo Emerson, Frank Furness was certainly no stranger to these ideas.

Since, for Ruskin, architectural beauty was to be found in ornamental details, he rarely illustrated or discussed a building as a whole. This brings us to the third aspect of his influence. The *Stones of Venice,* as can be seen by a glance at its contents page, isolates the individual parts of a building and treats them separately. Ruskin's architectural sketches are vignettes that concentrate upon individual features. The illustrations in the *Seven Lamps* (fig. 3), the *Stones,* and in such Ruskin-inspired works as George Edmund Street's *Brick and Marble in the Middle Ages* (1855), are eclectic accumulations of heterogeneous details: arches of different sizes and shapes, selected from different monuments, built up of separate and contrasting polychromatic voussoirs, moldings, and carved ornament, all jammed together within the confines of one framed page (fig. 4). The visual characteristics of the plates in these publications, this perception of a building as a cacophony of disjointed groupings of selected elements, was taken over wholesale by the architects of the Victorian Gothic years. Frank Furness was no exception.

Backed by the Ecclesiological Society, William Butterfield developed these characteristics at All Saints', Margaret Street, piling feature upon feature into an eclectic, picturesque, asymmetrical composition that is more animated than anything Ruskin had in mind, but nonetheless seemed like a brilliant application of his vision.[22]

All Saints' (fig. 5) combines nave, spire, and vestry into a dramatic, three-dimensional play of masses across the void of the entrance court. This compositional drama is reinforced inside and out by the application of varying colors, textures, material, patterns, and carved ornament, all overlaid—when the sun shines through London fog—by a shifting play of highlight and shadow.

5 William Butterfield. All Saints', Margaret Street, London. 1849–59 (from *The Builder,* 1853)

21. "This love of the beautiful in nature has been increasing from the most ancient times to the present. It is more generally felt and more fully enjoyed now than ever before, and in this country, apparently, more than in any other . . . ." G. B. Emerson, "What We Owe to Louis Agassiz as a Teacher," Address to the Boston Society of Natural History, January 7, 1874, p. 11 (printed copy in the Boston Athenaeum). Cf. Leo Marx, *The Machine in the Garden,* New York, 1964.

22. Paul Thompson, "All Saints' Church," *Architectural History,* VIII, 1965, pp. 73–95.

Surface and silhouette are activated by every means. On the exterior, spire opposes nave opposes vestry opposes buttress opposes wall opposes window opposes aedicule. The interior is a potpourri of richly colored materials bathed in colored light. Nor is nature excluded. Natural form is copied in ornamental details, and the microcosm of nature herself is introduced in the fossil-laden stones of the communion rail and baptismal font.

This colorful, dynamic interplay of rich and varied elements asymmetrically piled into picturesque conglomerates enriched by natural ornament is the essential characteristic of the architecture of the third phase of the Gothic Revival. That it is Gothic is almost incidental.[23] That it is often derivative in its elements is less important than that it is more often amazingly creative, original, and effective in its combination of these inherited details. At All Saints', later at Keble College in Oxford (1873), in building after building by Butterfield and others between the 1850s and the 1870s, this characteristic is essentially present.[24]

In the *Stones of Venice* Ruskin says of the Gothic *window* that it is "the best and strongest building" and pleads for the use of Gothic in domestic architecture because "it is the only form of faithful, strong, enduring, and honorable building." The ethical-poetical basis of Ruskin's fragmented Gothicism is clear here and stands in sharp contrast to the rationalism of E.-E. Viollet-le-Duc, chief French theoretician of the Gothic Revival.[25] Although completely different in basis and application, Viollet-le-Duc's theory of architecture also had a major impact upon European and American building.

Viollet-le-Duc was no less verbose than Ruskin, although less impassioned. Again we must restrict ourselves to a few salient ideas. Whereas Ruskin saw architecture as ornament, Viollet-le-Duc saw architecture as structure. As John Summerson has shown,[26] Viollet-le-Duc developed a rational interpretation of Gothic architecture in his multivolume *Dictionnaire raisonné de l'architecture française* of 1854–68, then turned criticism into theory in his *Entretiens sur l'architecture*, which appeared in two volumes in 1863 and 1872. The first volume of the *Entretiens* was translated into English as *The Discourses on Architecture* by Henry Van Brunt in 1875. Viollet-le-Duc shared Ruskin's demand for honesty in architecture, but where the Englishman saw Gothic as symbolic and associative, the Frenchman saw it as a logical structural system applicable, with significant changes in material, to nineteenth-century building needs. Every element in the Gothic system had its purpose; even the pinnacles served as counterweights to the diagonal vault thrusts. If such a logical statical system could be translated into iron, the characteristic material of the nineteenth century, a new architectural style would emerge based upon the superb equilibrium of Gothic architecture and the frank exposing of the superior strength of metal. So Viollet-le-Duc argued throughout the *Discourses*, applying the idea in various illustrations of the powerful, if awkward, hybrids he proposed (figs. 6, 7, 35, 37). These had great appeal to Furness.

Although Viollet-le-Duc based his theory of iron architecture upon Gothic principles, he did not restrict himself to that style in the designs illustrated in his *Discourses*. French architecture since the sixteenth century had been predominantly classical, and this tradition was still strong in the nineteenth century. Viollet's plates show metallic construction combined with the rectilinear organization of enriched and angular decorative details taken out of the French

6 E.-E. Viollet-le-Duc. "Maçonnerie" (from *Entretiens sur l'architecture: Atlas*, 1864, Pl. XX)

7 E.-E. Viollet-le-Duc. "Maçonnerie" (from *Entretiens: Atlas*, 1864, Pl. XIX)

23. It was not, of course, incidental to the Ecclesiologists. But the perspectives of time, enjoyed by the modern critic, and of distance, enjoyed by the American architect of the post-Civil War period, cool the heat of the battle of styles.

24. Hersey, *Victorian Gothic*; Robert F. Jordan, *Victorian Architecture*, Baltimore, 1966; John Summerson, *Victorian Architecture*, New York, 1970; Stefan Muthesius, *The High Victorian Movement in Architecture 1850–1870*, London and Boston, 1972.

25. Cf. Nikolaus Pevsner, *Ruskin and Viollet-le-Duc*, London, 1969.

26. John Summerson, "Viollet-le-Duc and the Rational Point of View," in his *Heavenly Mansions*, London, 1949 (paperback ed., New York, 1963), pp. 135 ff.

classical tradition (fig. 6). An architect need not have been a confirmed Gothicist to profit from Viollet-le-Duc's provocative designs.

In his use of classical details Viollet had something in common with his "Néo-Grec" contemporaries. Néo-Grec architects used classical details such as consoles, roundels, and channeled "triglyphs"—wrenched out of their original context and placed into an interwoven rectangular framework of pilasters and belt courses—to create buildings as picturesquely eclectic as anything in contemporary English Gothic work. Nor did Néo-Grec architects shun the use of iron. Henri Labrouste's Bibliothèque Ste. Geneviève of 1843–50 surrounds interior arched-iron construction with a classical masonry envelope decorated with Greek motifs. Close inspection of the interior of this building, well known to American Francophiles,[27] or the plates in Viollet's *Discourses* (fig. 7) reveals an ornamental use of abstract floral patterns based upon Greek precedent that is parallel to the work of Owen Jones across the Channel. There is a mid-century attitude toward ornamented surfaces that transcends national styles.[28]

Official patronage in Second Empire France favored the traditional classical style of pavilions, piled orders, mansard roofs, and heavy sculptural details that marks such major works as the New Louvre (1852–57), erected under the supervision of H. M. Lefuel and L. T. J. Visconti (fig. 8).[29] Although usually monochromatic, the plastic surfaces of these buildings become animated with the play of highlight and shadow causing them, too, to share the surface qualities characteristic of all mid-century work.

This more traditional French classical style is commonly associated with the government school of architecture, the École des Beaux-Arts. The École was a bad name to Bauhaus educational reformers and International Style modernists of the 1920s and 1930s, although they had learned more than they cared to admit from its teachings. In this century mention of it has conjured up visions of impractical and unbuildable projects: ink-wash renderings of buildings unrelated to real human needs, massive in size, axial in plan, and covered with a frosting of Baroque classical detail—all created for the sole purpose of winning the coveted Rome Prize. But the basic educational aim of the École was to teach design fundamentals. Its method was based upon the rational principles of planning, design, and construction summarized by Julien Guadet (himself a student at the École in the early 1860s) in his *Éléments et théorie d'architecture* of 1902.[30] École training became the main inspiration for architectural education in the United States after the Civil War. Even before the war, when Frank Furness began his studies, several Americans had attended the school. Among them—in fact, the first to go—was Richard Morris Hunt, and through Hunt, Furness himself came indirectly under its influence.

### 3. New York and Hunt (1859–61)

Furness's principal architectural training came during the years he spent in the atelier of Richard Morris Hunt (1827–1895) in New York. When Furness joined the atelier Hunt was in his early thirties, a dashing figure, and an inspiring draftsman and teacher.[31] He had just returned from Paris where he had studied at the École des Beaux-Arts in the late 1840s, and in the mid-1850s worked with Hector Lefuel on the New Louvre, supervising the construction (and certainly influencing the design) of the Pavillon de la Biblio-

8 Richard M. Hunt, for Hector Lefuel. Pavillon de la Bibliothèque, Louvre, Paris. 1852–55 (from *L'Architecture et la décoration aux Palais du Louvre et des Tuileries*, I, n.d., Pl. LXXIII)

27. It was extensively published and discussed during the 1850s, especially in César Daly's *Revue générale de l'architecture,* a periodical, we shall see, that was available to Furness as a student.

28. As Montgomery Schuyler put it in his essay on Hunt, the Néo-Grec "professed to offer the reconciliation of the classicism of the schools with the new romantic impulse." *American Architecture and Other Writings,* eds. William Jordy and Ralph Coe, 2 vols., Cambridge, Mass., 1961, II, p. 516.

29. The story is simplified here, too. For a more complete survey see Henry-Russell Hitchcock, *Architecture: Nineteenth and Twentieth Centuries,* 3d ed., Baltimore, 1968 (first paperback ed., 1971).

30. Reyner Banham, *Theory and Design in the First Machine Age,* London, 1960, pp. 15ff., 35ff.

31. Burnham, "Hunt," *JSAH,* XI, May 1952, pp. 9 ff.

9 Henry Van Brunt. Interior of Hunt's atelier, Studio Building, New York, April 1858. Courtesy William A. Coles

thèque (fig. 8). He returned to the States in 1855, the best trained architect in the country, and after a brief period with Thomas Ustick Walter in Washington, established himself in New York. For the next forty years Hunt occupied a place at the top of his profession in America, providing fashionable, French-inspired residences for nouveaux riches, such as the Vanderbilts, in New York, Newport, and North Carolina. As we shall see, Frank Furness learned more than just architectural design from this remarkable man.

It was late in 1857 or early in 1858 when Charles Gambrill, Henry Van Brunt, and George Post took quarters in Hunt's recently finished Studio Building on West Tenth Street. They were later joined by, among others, William Robert Ware (1832–1915) and Frank Furness. All five of these men were to become leading architects in the years following the Civil War: Gambrill, the least important, as the partner (1867–78) of H. H. Richardson; Van Brunt and Post as the designers of major buildings in Boston, New York, and the Middle West; Ware as educator and first professor of architecture at Massachusetts Institute of Technology (which established the first college-affiliated, professional school of architecture in this country in 1865); Furness as one of Philadelphia's leading architects from the early 1870s on. The influence of Hunt's atelier upon post-Civil War architecture can not be overestimated. First, American architecture as a profession was born in New York in the 1850s (the American Institute of Architects was established there in 1857 with Hunt a co-founder and first secretary). Second, the pedagogical method Hunt imported from Paris became the backbone of architectural education in this country until the diaspora of German artists and intellectuals under Hitler brought here the teachings of Gropius's Bauhaus in the late 1930s. Ware, who first at M.I.T. and later at Columbia formulated the academic program that dominated American architecture for more than half a century, wrote to Furness in 1898 that his "establishment" at Columbia was "a direct outcome of the 10th Street Studio of thirty-nine years ago."[32]

We are well informed about life and work in Hunt's atelier from two memoirs, one by Van Brunt published in full, the other by Furness himself published only in part.[33] The students were surrounded and inspired by Hunt's unrivaled collection of books, objets d'art, photographs, drawings, casts, and architectural ornament. The atelier was in fact an eclectic *Kunst- und Wunderkammer.* It presaged the standard setting for architectural drafting rooms for the next century. But in Hunt's atelier these objects did not serve merely as a backdrop, for the students studied them keenly. They formed an integral part of Hunt's method, which was based upon a thorough grounding in draftsmanship and modeled upon, but not restricted to, French methods and sources.

"In addition to the study of Orders," Furness recalled later in life,

> we were given each month a problem, which we first sketched and then worked up. . . . If the work was not finished . . . he gave us another problem; what he declared however to be most important was to "Draw, draw, draw! sketch, sketch, sketch! If you can't draw anything else, draw your boots, it doesn't matter, it will ultimately give you a certain control of your pencil so that you can the more rapidly express on paper your thoughts in designing. The greater facility you have in expressing those thoughts, the freer and better your designs will be."

And draw they did! Sketchbooks by Van Brunt, preserved from his Studio

32. Letter in possession of George Wood Furness. See also Section 9.

33. See note 13. Van Brunt's memoir is conveniently found in William A. Coles, ed., *Architecture and Society,* Cambridge, Mass., 1969, pp. 328 ff. It was written in 1895. See also the preface to William Robert Ware's *American Vignola,* Scranton, Pa., 1905.

days, contain a visual record of his surroundings (fig. 9) as well as architectural studies based upon plates from various books in Hunt's library (fig. 10). These were mostly French, as we would expect, although an occasional English and German author appears as well.[34] A sample listing of publications includes works by Thomas Rickman, Jean LePautre, Ludwig Runge, Victor Petit, Israël Silvestre, Alexandre de Laborde, and especially, César Daly's periodical *Revue générale de l'architecture*. Nor is it possible that Viollet-le-Duc was overlooked.[35] Furness's own gifted draftsmanship, which we assume was in evidence prior to his study in New York, flowered under such intense training. At the same time he stored away a wide variety of useful English and French details.

Sketching was only one means to an end; the study of precedent was another. The classical orders were fundamental, as Furness wrote:

> The first thing he required . . . was to learn thoroughly the Orders of Architecture, so thoroughly that if he gave us a moulding taken from any one of the different Orders, we could construct . . . the entire order.
>
> He was most decided in his opinion that everyone should be thoroughly trained in the Orders; He used to say: "No matter if you never practice classical architecture, you acquire a certain idea or instinct of proportion that will never leave you, and that is essential to good designing in any of the different schools."

Van Brunt's memoir makes clear how Hunt instructed his students to use these fundamental elements:

> Hunt ever insisted upon the pre-eminent importance of academical discipline and order in design. He was most concerned that the sub-structure of our knowledge should be serious, sane and solid. We were instructed to make our plans on rigidly scholastic lines, and the vertical developments in the elevations we were taught to study in strict classic form according to the method of the French school. Respect for authority and discipline was thus inculcated. . . . But while he insisted on the preservation of the classic formulas for the sake of the training of mind and hand, he heartily encouraged the study of every style in which the thought of man has expressed itself in beauty or power.

The classical system was basic, then, but Furness and Van Brunt outline a tolerant, eclectic approach to architectural design. All of the past, classical and medieval alike, was available for picturesque compositions, as were more recent French and English sources. Such eclecticism could be justified by the Victorian theory of progress. In the introduction to his translation of Viollet-le-Duc's *Discourses*, for example, Van Brunt put the case in a nutshell:

> It must not be forgotten that the most essential distinction between the arts of primitive barbarism and those of civilization is that, while the former are original and independent, and consequently simple, the latter must be retrospective, naturally turning to tradition and precedent, and are therefore complex. A beginning once made by primitive discovery . . . art . . . must thenceforward proceed by derivation and development; and where architectural monuments and traditions have accumulated to the vast extent that they have in modern times, the question is not whether we shall use them at all, but how shall we choose among them, and to what extent shall such choice be allowed to influence our modern practice.[36]

10 Henry Van Brunt. Drawings after Victor Petit. c. 1858–59. Courtesy William A. Coles

34. W. A. Coles, "Richard Morris Hunt and His Library," *Art Quarterly*, XXX, Fall/Winter 1967, pp. 225 ff.

35. According to the contemporary New York architect P. B. Wight, R. M. Hunt was "at one time . . . largely influenced by the teachings of Viollet-le-Duc, and the example of Ruprich Robert and Henri Labrouste" (*Inland Architect*, XXVI, August 1895, p. 4). We return to all three of these Frenchmen in the text below.

36. Coles, *Architecture and Society*, p. 103. Van Brunt is referring specifically to "we Americans." Eclecticism or historicism was also supported by associationism. The more details borrowed from the more sources, the more associative information a building could convey. See Hersey, *Victorian Gothic*.

11 Frank Furness. Caricatures. Sketchbook drawing (detail). Collection George Wood Furness

IS IT A NIGHTMARE OR ONLY A CRAMP

SOO BIG

12 Frank Furness. "IS IT A NIGHTMARE OR ONLY A CRAMP." Sketchbook drawing. Collection George Wood Furness

37. Paul Thompson, *William Butterfield,* Cambridge, Mass., 1971, chap. 7.

38. Including H. S. Goodhart-Rendel's "Rogue Architects of the Victorian Era," *Journal of the Royal Institute of British Architects,* 3d ser., XLVIII, 1949, pp. 251 ff.

39. *Records of a Lifelong Friendship,* between pp. 102 and 103; for a caricature by Horace, see Jayne, *Letters of Horace Howard Furness,* p. 41.

40. See note 61.

41. Perhaps the foremost New York architect of the 1850s, and first president of the A.I.A., Richard Upjohn should be mentioned, too, although there seems to be no connection between his work and that of Furness.

For an English Victorian Gothic architect, eclecticism or historicism usually meant selecting from the medieval past.[37] For the French Néo-Grec architect, eclecticism usually meant rearranging the details of classical architecture. But in Hunt's atelier, and so in his work and that of his students, English medievalism and French classicism merged. In its combination of these influences much American architecture of the post–Civil War years is unique. The work of Frank Furness has no real parallel in Europe.[38] While the picturesque was a general international style and Furness's borrowed details can be spotted in the European originals, his mature work was neither Gothic nor Néo-Grec, but an original amalgam of the two.

Life in the atelier was not all work. It would be wrong to leave this period in Furness's life without mentioning another aspect of his talent that manifested itself there. The art of caricature seems to have run in the Furness family. The oldest brother (like his ancestor John Mason Furnass) was a professional portrait draftsman, and both Dr. Furness and Horace Howard were given now and then to sketching friends and acquaintances with exaggerated features. A caricature of Henry David Thoreau, for example, appears in a letter of 1854 from Dr. Furness to Emerson.[39] But the muse of physiognomical distortion seems to have found particular expression through Frank, and not without occasional comical and embarrassing consequences, especially in the Studio days. Hunt, according to Furness, entered the atelier one morning to find Frank

at the blackboard engaged in drawing a rough caricature of Quincy. . . . unconscious of Mr. Hunt's presence [I] went on drawing, although dimly aware that my drawing did not seem to be meeting with as loud applause as when I first began. All of a sudden I was horrorstruck at the sound of Mr. Hunt's voice exclaiming "Great God! Furness, if you can only caricature a plan as well as you can Quincy, and get as much ink on paper as you have on your coat, you will be a Michael Angelo." I dropped the chalk and tried . . . to sneak to my drawing board, but it was not to be. Mr. Hunt kept me at the blackboard making attempts at caricaturing the whole party, including himself.

Furness was apparently not entirely proud of his ability to render people ridiculous, for he ends this account with an assessment of his talent:

Thereafter I was frequently ordered to the blackboard to finish off the hour of daily instruction by showing, as it appears to me, how badly a man can draw and yet produce some slight resemblance to the individual.

The Furness sketchbooks are filled with caricatures of himself, his family, his acquaintances and his clients,[40] ranging from the superb to the sophomoric to the vicious (figs. 11, 12). Though he thought little of his ability, he seems to have exercised it a great deal over a long period of time. There is a family tradition that it added to his later reputation as a disagreeable character.

A student of architecture absorbs not only what his teacher tells him in the drafting room or points out to him in the library: he is naturally curious about the buildings his teacher is designing, as well as those of his teacher's fellow architects. It must be expected that Furness's education in architecture was not confined to the Studio, but extended to the streets of New York where he and his fellow neophytes could sharpen their critical eyes—and tongues too, probably—on the work of Hunt, of Leopold Eidlitz, of Detlef Lienau, and of other architectural leaders of the city in the late 1850s including, if not especially, Jacob Wrey Mould.[41] New York in the fifties reflected the major currents of European architecture, especially High Victorian and Second Empire, and outside the atelier as well as within Furness breathed the air of both.

Hunt's first American work, the E. K. Rossiter House of 1855–57, was thoroughly French and thoroughly Second Empire.[42] Its Renaissance detail included, at the portals, the French national order invented in the late sixteenth century by Philibert de l'Orme. This was as close to Paris as Furness ever got, unless one counts the Studio Building itself—a rectangular paneled brick façade with large, segmental-headed windows and patterned brick cornice. Such rectangular surface articulation appears often in Hunt's work—and Furness's too, since Hunt remained a prime source of ideas for Furness, even in the seventies and eighties.

Detlef Lienau (1818–1887) was German trained and had worked in Paris with Henri Labrouste[43]; he arrived in New York in 1848. His town house for the French banker Hart M. Shiff, with its flat rectangular brick façades and mansard roof, was as French as anything Shiff could have found in Paris and preceded Hunt's Rossiter House by five years. It would have attracted Hunt's students, as would, even more, Lienau's more recent Schermerhorn House, finished in May of 1859, at just about the moment Furness entered the Studio. The Schermerhorn House was no less French than the Rossiter, although less aggressively so. Again, flat rectangularity dominated the façade.[44]

Leopold Eidlitz (1823–1908), Prague-born and Vienna-trained, arrived in New York five years before Lienau.[45] His several New York works of the 1850s also must have attracted the notice of the Studio, but more importantly, in 1859 he and Van Brunt exchanged views in print on the use of iron in architecture, an exchange that no doubt became a topic of conversation in the atelier. Later buildings by Eidlitz, whose reputation grew in the sixties and seventies, were to be particularly useful to Furness.[46]

Other than Hunt himself, the architect active in New York in the 1850s who seems to have appealed the most to Furness was Jacob Wrey Mould (1825–1886), an Englishman who arrived in 1853.[47] In Mould's All Souls' Unitarian Church of 1853–55—especially in the original project with spire and even more in the elevation of the parsonage, with its huge traceried, round-arched window supported by crude corbels that overwhelms the simple gabled façade (fig. 13)—we first encounter the direct impact of Ruskin and Butterfield in America, and the first flickering of the kind of architectural design Furness would produce after the war. The fact that Mould had worked in England for the master of polychromy, Owen Jones, insured that these works would be rich in coloration. And the fact that All Souls' was a Unitarian church for H. W. Bellows, a friend of Dr. Furness, makes it highly possible that Furness knew well this and other works by Mould, as David Van Zanten has suggested. The ornament developed by Mould in New York, based upon nature and the principles outlined by Owen Jones in his *Grammar of Ornament* (1856), was to be one important source of Furness's own decorative style.

In New York artistic circles in the late 1850s it would have been very easy (almost unavoidable) to come into contact with other English ideas. A Ruskinian art journal called the *Crayon,* begun in 1855, published the exchange of views between Van Brunt and Eidlitz on the use of iron. And 1857 saw the exhibition of many works of the Pre-Raphaelite Brotherhood. The presence of England was as prevalent as that of France.[48]

13 Jacob Wrey Mould. All Souls' Parsonage, New York. 1853–55

42. See note 31.

43. Helen W. Kramer, "Detlef Lienau," *JSAH,* XIV, March 1955, pp. 18 ff.

44. It is not just Lienau's work of the 1850s that should be remembered in connection with Furness: there are parallels in their postwar work. Lienau's Lockwood House in Norwalk, Conn., of the late 1860s, for example, bears comparison to Furness's work of the 1870s, especially the central, top-lighted well of space, the fireplace with opening above, and the Néo-Grec ornamentation.

45. Schuyler, *American Architecture,* I, pp. 21 ff., 136 ff.

46. See below, and note 91.

47. D. T. Van Zanten, "Jacob Wrey Mould," *JSAH,* XXVIII, March 1969, pp. 41 ff.

48. See D. H. Dickason, *The Daring Young Men,* Bloomington, Ind., 1953; R. B. Stein, *John Ruskin and Aesthetic Thought in America,* Cambridge, Mass., 1967; and H.-R. Hitchcock, "Ruskin and American Architecture," *Concerning Architecture,* ed. J. Summerson, London, 1968, pp. 166 ff.

Plate 2 Pennsylvania Academy of the Fine Arts.  Broad Street elevation, by Furness and Hewitt.  1873.
Ink and wash on paper.  Pennsylvania Academy of the Fine Arts, Philadelphia

Plate 3 Pennsylvania Academy of the Fine Arts.  Broad Street façade

14 Leopold Eidlitz. Temple Emanu-El, New York. 1866–68. Courtesy Congregation Emanu-El, New York

Iron was used—and its use debated—in New York in the fifties. On the Laing Stores of 1849 James Bogardus placed cast-iron fronts designed after an Italian Renaissance *palazzo*. Van Brunt objected to what he viewed as such misuse of iron in imitation of stone. In his paper he called for a "cast iron architecture" to express the "cast iron age."[49] Old forms should be modified to accommodate them to the new material. This did not mean that precedent should be neglected. Progress in architecture is made not by the invention of new forms, but by the subtle growth of new things out of old. Styles of the past that lend themselves to adaptation in iron should be selected. It is easy to see why Van Brunt was sufficiently attracted to Viollet-le-Duc to translate his *Discourses*. Furness certainly heard Van Brunt's views in the atelier, and on the basis of his later work such as the University Library, we can guess that he shared them.

Furness's two years in New York introduced him to the major currents of European and American architectural thought—currents that were to continue to flow through the war years and beyond. When he returned to civilian life in 1864, he found the architectural scene a familiar one, and it developed along these same lines for many years.

## 4. England, France, and Philadelphia

In the 1860s and 1870s, while Furness was in the South or beginning architectural practice, American architecture clearly showed its dual imported sources. In New York in the 1860s the influence of Ruskin was paramount. The Society for the Advancement of Truth in Art was founded there in 1863 and began publishing a journal called the *New Path*. P. B. Wight's National Academy of Design of 1862–65 took the form of the Venetian Doge's Palace, Ruskin's favorite. Buildings such as the Temple Emanu-El of 1866–68 (fig. 14) or the Church of the Holy Family of 1870–75, both by Leopold Eidlitz, evoked all the polychromatic drama of the High Victorian Gothic in England; in fact, the strident surface coloration of the Holy Family earned it the popular name of the "Homely Oilcloth."

But the influence of Second Empire Paris grew apace. In Washington in 1859 James Renwick began the Corcoran Gallery, and in Boston in 1862 the architects Gridley J. F. Bryant and Arthur Gilman began Old City Hall. These were the earliest of the monumental French-inspired buildings in the States, but not the last. After the war the Second Empire became the quasi-official governmental style, and the architect of the U.S. Treasury, A. B. Mullett, spread French taste from the State, War and Navy Building in Washington, D.C. (1871), to the old Post Office in St. Louis (1874) to the U.S. Mint in San Francisco (1870).

Not all American buildings of these years fall easily into one camp or the other. Harvard's Memorial Hall, inspired by Ruskin's friend Charles Eliot Norton, draws ideas from both sources. Designed immediately after the war by Ware and Van Brunt and erected between 1870 and 1878, the structure is actually three "buildings" in one. Using the analytical planning method we associate with the Parisian École, the architects combined dining hall, memorial proper, and theater into a vaguely ecclesiastical, richly colorful envelope with the energized silhouette characteristic of English building. Van Brunt, who was translating Viollet-le-Duc's *Discourses* as the building rose, used exposed trusses above the dining hall and the exterior wall buttresses that receive them to express honestly the working structure, thus combining the ideas of both Ruskin and Viollet.

49. "Cast Iron in Decorative Architecture," in Coles, *Architecture and Society*, pp. 77 ff.

The two strains are evident in Philadelphia itself in the years following the war. The uniformity of the "Quaker style" gave way before the richness of the new architecture.[50] Thomas Richard's College Hall at the new University of Pennsylvania in West Philadelphia, begun early in 1871, with its (originally) towered silhouette and green Serpentine walls is a local variant on the Victorian Gothic; while McArthur's City Hall is still the city's most conspicuous Francophile structure, although its richness of surface *and* silhouette show that he was interested in the English picturesque as well.

It is still possible in Philadelphia to form some idea of the picturesque urban result of mingling the two national sources by standing in front of Furness's Pennsylvania Academy on North Broad and looking south toward City Hall tower (fig. 1). Joining it in a multipronged vignette of about 1870 are the Arch Street Methodist Church of 1868 by Addison Hutton and the Masonic Temple of 1867–73 by James Windrim. The latter is "Norman Romanesque" in style but has all the animation of surface and silhouette we associate with High Victorian Gothic. It carried on the round-arched picturesqueness that existed in Philadelphia even before the war in such Romanesque buildings as John Notman's Holy Trinity Church of 1857–59 (the tower later). Viewed against these buildings, Furness's work of the 1870s and later appears strikingly personal in its interpretation of the available source material.

## 5. Fraser, Furness and Hewitt (1867–71)

In 1866 Furness designed a simple cruciform stone Gothic church for the Unitarian Society of Germantown (fig. 15); the commission presumably came to him through his father's connections.[51] He apparently executed this work by himself, but by 1867 had formed a partnership and, with the exception of a few years in the late 1870s, his work from then on was done in association with others. Although it is not always easy to be specific about his contributions and those of the members of his changing and expanding firm, there is nothing to suggest that Furness in his prime was not in complete control of design.

His first partnership included his former employer, John Fraser (c. 1825–1903?), and an architect of his own generation, George W. Hewitt (1841–1916)—a partnership that lasted until Fraser moved to Washington, D.C., in 1871.[52] Fraser's Union League Club of 1864–65 on South Broad Street is a red brick and brownstone block with sweeping front stairs, mansard roof, and (originally) an asymmetrical tower. French, although hardly French enough to satisfy Furness's training, and modified by English picturesque massing, the Union League must have attracted Furness back to his former boss. George Hewitt was not committed to French sources. He had worked for John Notman in the six years before Notman's death in 1865, and in 1868 erected the tower of Notman's Holy Trinity Church on Rittenhouse Square.

The Church of the Holy Apostles at Twenty-first and Christian streets was commissioned early in 1868 (cat. 1). Nominally by the firm of Fraser, Furness and Hewitt, it was mainly by George Hewitt and forms a crucial link between the prewar work of Notman and the more colorful buildings of the postwar years. Holy Apostles, like Holy Trinity, is an asymmetrically towered stone Romanesque building, but the polychromatic alternating voussoirs of its exterior arches, with their round intrados and pointed extrados, give just a faint hint of things to come (plate 1). So does the elaborate (and badly engineered) wood trusswork supporting the high gable roof inside (cat. 1-3).

15 Frank Furness. Unitarian Church, Germantown, Philadelphia. 1866–67. Courtesy Unitarian Church, Germantown, Philadelphia

50. For the Philadelphia buildings in this essay see George B. Tatum, *Penn's Great Town*, Philadelphia, 1961; and Theo B. White, ed., *Philadelphia Architecture in the Nineteenth Century*, Philadelphia, 1953.

51. Documentation for Furness's works will be found either in the catalogue or the checklist accompanying this essay.

52. The partnership was dissolved on September 1, 1871, according to a letter of October 5 from Fraser to John Sartain in the Archives of the Pennsylvania Academy. There are few available data concerning Fraser's career (I am indebted to Richard Derman for his work on Fraser); for Hewitt see his obituary in the *A.I.A. Journal*, August 1916, p. 361.

Without doubt the most auspicious example of the firm's work was the German synagogue, Rodef Shalom, of 1869 (cat. 2). A single-naved, gable-roofed, red brick building animated on the exterior by an asymmetrical bulb-topped tower, Gothic and Islamic arches built up of alternating brick and stone voussoirs, Gothic-inspired carved details, iron ridge crestings and other exotica of polychrome picturesque architecture—this early collaborative effort is often given to Hewitt alone, but it contained many details characteristic of Furness's later work. The horseshoe arches of vaguely Eastern derivation were common touches in synagogue design in the nineteenth century, but Furness himself would use them in later works for the Jewish community, notably in the hospital on North Broad Street, as well as in the Brazilian Pavilion and the Zoo Restaurant. And the rather timid aedicules crowning the gables would become a major skyline feature on the First Unitarian Church.

The horseshoe arch was carried into the interior of Rodef Shalom in the window openings, the wide-spaced scalloped trefoil wood trusses and the arches dividing the open nave from the tabernacle at one end, and the recess above the vestibule at the other (cat. 2-1). These arches were supported on two tiers of stubby scagliola columns resting on consoles. A gallery on brackets ran down either side of the nave, repeating a feature used in the Holy Apostles. The interior of black walnut, butternut, and bright stenciled ornament, enriched by colored light from the painted glass, focused upon the baldachino, or tabernacle, at the east end (cat. 2-3). This echoed the bulb-topped tower of the exterior and was itself the origin of the corner porch Furness later used at the First Unitarian.

Rodef Shalom was, in all respects, a building characteristic of its time, place, and use. In its unbalanced massing and surface richness it showed that Furness and his partners were on the same path in the late 1860s as most other American and English architects. It can be compared, for example, with its New York counterpart, Eidlitz's Temple Emanu-El (fig. 14). Furness or Hewitt probably traveled to New York to study this just-finished building when they received their synagogue commission. The great scalloped arches supported by columns on consoles that spanned the nave of Emanu-El were repeated at Rodef Shalom, although Furness with characteristic overstatement doubled his supports.[53] Furness and Hewitt were to recall Emanu-El again at the Pennsylvania Academy.

## 6. Furness and Hewitt (1871-75)

In 1871 John Fraser moved to Washington where he became acting supervising architect of the Treasury Department. Furness and Hewitt continued to practice for four years, until Hewitt too left to form another partnership (in 1878) with his brother William. It was during these years that the firm received its first important commission and established its national reputation. And it was during these years that a young wiseacre named Louis Sullivan came down from Boston to work briefly for the firm in its office across from the (now-demolished) Jayne Building on Chestnut Street.[54]

From Sullivan and other sources we have a remarkable portrait of the partners at this time. Despite the fact that fifty years had passed, Sullivan recalled both Furness and Hewitt vividly when he sat down as a disgruntled old man to write his Autobiography in the early 1920s. He had been told in New York to look

53. The interior of Emanu-El appeared in *Frank Leslie's Illustrated Newspaper* for October 3, 1868, p. 41 (reproduced in Schuyler, *American Architecture*, I, p. 158).

54. Louis H. Sullivan, *The Autobiography of an Idea*, New York, 1949, pp. 190 ff.

up the firm once he arrived—all of sixteen years old that summer of 1873—but scouted its buildings first, finding a house by the firm on South Broad that was "something fresh and fair . . . , a human note, as though someone were talking." The next day he went to Furness and Hewitt to announce that he would work for them, "they to have no voice in the matter." Sullivan's description of the thirty-four-year-old Furness, whom he found a "curious character," is worth quoting at length:

> He affected the English in fashion . . . wore loud plaids, and a scowl, and from his face depended fan-like a marvellous red beard. . . . his face was snarled and homely as an English bulldog's. Louis's eyes were riveted, in infatuation, to this beard, as he listened to a string of oaths yards long.

Of the two partners Furness had obviously the stronger personality and intellect. The "dog-man," as Sullivan called him, "made buildings out of his head" and was an "extraordinary" draftsman. "He had Louis hypnotized, especially when he drew and swore at the same time." Furness's colorful use of language struck all who remembered him; he himself acknowledged a debt here to his teacher, Hunt. In his memoir, already quoted at length, Furness admitted that he tried to be like the "object of his enthusiasm," imitating as well as he could "Mr. Hunt's forcible manner of expressing himself."

> This was the only accomplishment acquired during my "apprenticeship" in Mr. Hunt's studio which proved of energetic efficacy in the army—especially useful to a cavalry officer. . . . On one occasion after my return to New York, when the responsibilities of the business were more or less committed to my charge . . . Some contractor or other had vexed me by what I considered his stupidity, . . . I "cut loose at him" for about one steady minute. The sliding doors were quickly pushed aside, and Mr. Hunt's face with a comical expression appeared in the opening. "Good heavens! Furness," he cried, "the pupil has surpassed the master in one respect at any rate!"[55]

And these accounts are confirmed by the memory of one of Furness's Philadelphia colleagues. According to Albert Kelsey,

> he was one of the most picturesque personalities I have ever known. . . . He could swear like a trooper. . . . To see him go down the street, with his shoulders squared, head erect, and with a free, swinging soldierly stride, and a devil-may-care attitude was to realize that here was a man who neither gave nor asked for quarter. . . . In all that he did . . . there was the impress of a masterful mind. . . . It was characteristic that in his dress he always wore the loudest and biggest plaids that he could find [fig. 16] . . . he wore his hat, with a rakish tilt over his eye. . . . In his . . . office he was a severe and strict disciplinarian but as ready in kindly counsel and friendly aid as he was quick to wrath and explosive anger over any exhibition of indifference or stupidity.[56]

Sullivan, Kelsey, and Furness himself present us with an extraordinarily consistent picture of a colorful personality fine-honed by military discipline, incapable of tolerating indifference or inability in the pursuit of excellence to which he himself was committed—yet capable of verbal expression as gifted and probably as original in composition as his architecture itself. He seems to have had a perpetual chip on his shoulder. A domineering presence such as this must have been hard to live with professionally, socially, and domestically.[57]

16 Frank Furness at his desk, 1880s. Courtesy George Wood Furness

55. This passage clearly indicates that Furness returned to Hunt's office after the war.

56. *Philadelphia Evening Bulletin,* April 18, 1924, p. 8, col. 5.

57. Of the innumerable anecdotes concerning Furness's cantankerous personality that still circulate in Philadelphia, one is worth repeating here. The artist Alfred Bendiner wrote to the *A.I.A. Journal* (July 1957, p. 207) that "Frank Lloyd Wright told me that Louis Sullivan told him that Furness told him that his great ambition in life was to get his clients into the Academy of Music so that he could come out on stage and tell them all to go to hell."

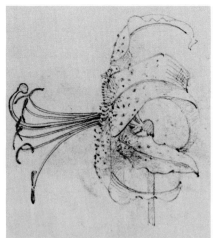

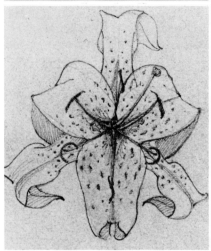

17 Frank Furness. Two drawings of a Turk's-Cap Lily. Sketchbook drawings. Collection George Wood Furness

58. This is confirmed by the drawings in the Academy collection. They show decorative details that were later changed or never executed (plate 2, cat. 3-8).

59. Frank's brother Horace credited Fairman Rogers with "much that is admirable and best" in the Academy's "internal design and arrangement." H[orace] H[oward] F[urness], *F[airman] R[ogers] 1833–1900,* Philadelphia, 1903, p. 13. John Sartain also claimed credit for the interior. "The designs submitted, . . . while pretty enough in exterior effect, were within altogether unsuited to the uses required, notwithstanding full printed instructions as to what was needed. So all were rejected . . . and the drawings returned to the owners. . . . I was then asked to prepare plans for the distribution of the class-rooms and galleries, irrespective of course of the architectural forms, which were the province of the architects selected, Messrs. Furness and Hewitt." John Sartain, *Reminiscences of a Very Old Man,* New York, 1899, p. 252.
The public museum was a relatively new architectural problem in this country in 1871. For a discussion of this building type in nineteenth-century America see Jay Cantor, "Temples of the Arts," *Metropolitan Museum of Art Bulletin,* April 1970, pp. 331–354; and Margaret Floyd's article on the Boston Museum of Fine Arts (designed 1870), scheduled to appear in *JSAH* for May 1973.
It was typical of Furness's commissions that influential people concerned with the building were

George Hewitt was, on the other hand, according to Sullivan,

> a slender, mustached person, pale and reserved, who seldom relaxed from his pose. It was he who did the Victorian Gothic in its pantalettes. . . . With precision . . . he worked out these decorous sublimities of inanity, as per the English current magazines and other English sources. He was a clean draftsman, and believed implicitly that all that was good was English.

Sullivan admired Hewitt as a draftsman yet held him in contempt "as a man who kept his nose in the books." So did Furness, but Sullivan's esteem for the man blinded him to Furness's own eclecticism. And an examination of Hewitt's later work reveals that if he lacked Furness's force, it was not to the degree that Sullivan would have us believe. However, the distinction Sullivan makes between the two men as designers and as personalities is a useful one. It is no surprise that the partnership lasted just four years.

By the fall, the depression of 1873 had hit the architectural offices and Sullivan, as the youngest member of the staff, was let go. He went on to Chicago, to Paris, and back to Chicago, eventually to occupy an important niche in American architectural history; but Furness had made a lasting impression upon him. Sullivan in retrospect gave thanks that he had been fortunate enough to have

> made his entry into the practical world in an office where standards were so high—where talent was so manifestly taken for granted, and the atmosphere the free and easy one of a true work shop savoring of the guild where craftsmanship was paramount and personal.

Sullivan worked for Furness at a time when the raw materials of the latter's style were still very apparent, and in the buildings erected with Hewitt before the middle of the seventies they can be distinguished with ease. After that date an amalgamation occurred, and Furness's own aggressive style clearly emerged.

The most important building rising from the designs of Furness and Hewitt while Sullivan was in the office was the Pennsylvania Academy of the Fine Arts, still standing on North Broad Street at the corner of Cherry (cat. 3). It would seem from Fairman Rogers's address at the laying of the cornerstone in December 1872 that the design was not yet established in all its details,[58] but the projected building was satisfactory to Dr. Furness, who also spoke. He was delighted to find that the "monotony of our [Quaker] streets is disappearing; the spirit of beauty is beginning to brood over our city, over its private dwellings and public edifices." Both Rogers and the senior Furness found that the finished building had lived up to their expectations when they returned to speak at the dedication ceremonies in April 1876.

The program dated June 20, 1871, was drawn up by a building committee including Rogers and John Sartain and sent to a limited number of local architects. It called for a two-story, fireproof building, having a flexible arrangement of top-lighted galleries of varying sizes on the upper floor, all accessible from the main stair; and a lower floor containing library, lecture room, galleries for casts, and a painting room well lighted from a window close to the ceiling. The main front was to be on Broad Street with a students' entrance off Cherry. The existing building follows this program very closely.[59] In the Furness and Hewitt design, studios and galleries stretch out along either side of a central corridor defined by brick walls that rise from basement to roof.

To the east this long rectangle develops into a monumental "façade-house" containing the impressive top-lighted stairhall. The fireproofing requirement resulted in a building constructed entirely of brick, stone, and iron (the latter for structural beams and roof trusses).

The Broad Street front (plates 2, 3) is a traditional tripartite composition of projecting central salient flanked by lower wings. It is, in fact, a "Victorianization" of the earlier, Neo-classical Academy building erected by R. A. Gilpin in 1846–47 and demolished in 1870. The central pavilion itself, however, with its mansard roof and pointed window, is a combination of motifs taken from Eidlitz's Victorian Gothic Temple Emanu-El in New York (fig. 14) and the Pavillon de la Bibliothèque at the Louvre (fig. 8), executed by R. M. Hunt and certainly well known to Furness. So the building is a mixture of English and French ideas. Although the richness of the exterior surfaces is primarily due to the influence of Venetian architecture via Ruskin and Butterfield, Néo-Grec organization and details are also present. These surfaces are broken into interlocking rectangular panels and activated by a busy variety of forms and materials: rusticated brownstone, dressed sandstone, polished granite, pointed and traceried arches, red pressed brick set in black mortar, diaper patterns laid in undulating red and black brick, painted glass, carved reliefs, floriated merlons, and on and on.[60] According to Sullivan we should ascribe all of the Anglophile features to Hewitt and reserve for Furness that which is French in the design. But the division is not that clear cut.

In the spandrels of the central archway and in the tympana of the pointed windows flanking the main pavilion (cat. 3-2); above the entrance on Cherry Street (cat. 3-3); in the form of the bronze light fixtures at the main entrance and on the main stairway (cat. 3-9); and throughout the interior of the building, we find carved, cut, cast, stenciled, punched, incised, or painted ornament in formalized floral patterns that are characteristic of Furness and Hewitt's work from Rodef Shalom on. Furness continued to use these abstract patterns in his independent work, although from the early 1880s he as frequently used very naturalistic foliage as well. This ornament was inspired by Ruskin but, especially in its conventionalized form, modified by other sources.

We recall that Ruskin had limited his definition of architecture to the embellishment of structure that produces beauty—beauty limited to the imitation of nature—and in the Oxford Museum he had ordered carved flora and fauna around the window openings from designs of the Pre-Raphaelite Brotherhood. Minute examination of natural form was the foundation of architectural ornament as long as the Ruskinian esthetic held sway in England and America. Furness followed suit. His sketchbooks are filled with drawing after drawing from nature: flowers, animals, landscapes keenly observed and duly recorded.[61] Just as Furness was not content merely to record the outward appearance of his friends and clients but probed deeper by means of caricature, so in his flower drawings, especially, he proceeded a step beyond the simple record. In several of the preserved drawings (fig. 17) flowers are rendered in "plan" and "elevation," showing their geometric symmetry like the working drawings for a building; in others he seemed to probe beyond external appearance to discover the underlying geometric pattern, the axes of growth, that gives them their unique form. Certainly this goes beyond anything recommended by Ruskin or the Pre-Raphaelites, but it is not without precedent.

18 Owen Jones. "Leaves and Flowers from Nature" (from *The Grammar of Ornament*, 1856, Pl. XCVIII)

part of, or associated with, Furness's family. Horace was a subscriber to the building fund. His father's addresses suggest that he was not a disinterested party. John Sartain was his father's friend, and had engraved many of the younger William's portraits at his death. Fairman Rogers was an in-law (Horace's wife was a Rogers).

60. The reliefs in place bear groups of figures extracted from Paul Delaroche's frescoed *Glorification of the Fine Arts* in the Hemicycle of the École des Beaux-Arts in Paris. The still uncarved square panels to right and left of the main window were to contain heads of Apelles and Phidias, according to the drawing of the building published in *Lippincott's* for March 1872. This also shows the Greek figure which stood for many years on the pedestal in front of the main window.

61. There are fifteen sketchbooks, of varying size and ranging in date from the early 1870s to the mid-1890s, in the possession of George Wood Furness. Their contents include caricatures; financial accounts; designs for furniture, jewelry, and ornament; landscape, plant, and animal studies; and architectural projects. Furness's drafting style apparently progressed from the nervous, broken-line technique he learned from Hunt to the smooth, continuous line he employed in the nineties.

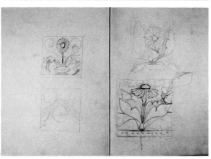

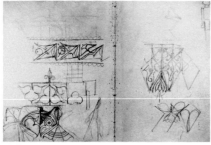

19 Frank Furness. Studies for architectural ornament. Sketchbook drawings. Collection George Wood Furness

62. "Building in Philadelphia," *AABN*, I, October 14, 1876, pp. 334–336.

63. Coles, *Architecture and Society*, Figs. 10, 11.

64. *Revue*, XI, 1853, cols. 241 ff. This volume contains a plate of foliate iron details from Labrouste's Bibliothèque Ste. Geneviève, details that must have caught Furness's fancy. His own punched-iron decoration owes much to them.

Owen Jones's *Grammar of Ornament* appeared in London in 1856. It contains a survey of historical styles, primarily intended to influence the ornament of the day. Jones was not satisfied with the mere replication of nature. He agreed with Ruskin that the ornamentalist should "return to Nature for fresh inspiration," but his propositions 8 and 13 state flatly that "all ornament should be based upon a geometrical construction," and that "flowers or other natural objects should not be used as ornaments, but conventional representations founded upon them sufficiently suggestive to convey the intended image to the mind. . . ." A comparison of Jones's Plate XCVIII (fig. 18) with Furness's "architectural" drawings of a Turk's-cap lily (fig. 17) is enough to convince us that Furness knew the Englishman's work. Jones wrote that the plate illustrates "several varieties of flowers, in plan and elevation, from which it will be seen that the basis of all form is geometry, the impulse which forms the surface, starting from the centre with equal force, necessarily stops at equal distances; the result is symmetry and regularity." The symmetrical, conventionalized, almost abstract floral patterns above the side windows of the Academy's Broad Street front (cat. 3-2) demonstrate Furness's application of Jones's rules of ornament, as do several pages of studies for ornament in the sketchbooks of this period (fig. 19).

Furness's training was French oriented. Where did he run into the work of Owen Jones? A writer discussing Furness's architecture (including the Academy) in the *American Architect* for October 14, 1876, significantly compared it to that of Jacob Wrey Mould:

> Both are wonderfully fertile and brilliant in invention, with a keen delight in color, which sometimes makes them forget that architecture is essentially an art of modelling with lights and shadows. The most brilliant performances of both are in picturesque, rather than in monumental designs; . . . the decorator in them tends to overpower the architect.[62]

Mould had worked for Jones in England and designed a Unitarian church in New York for a friend of Dr. Furness, so there can be little doubt that Mould introduced the young Furness to Jones's theory of architectural ornament, recently published when Furness arrived in New York.

Yet the path to Jones led probably not only through Mould's work but through the pages of César Daly's *Revue générale de l'architecture* as well. We know that this periodical was in Hunt's atelier because Van Brunt copied monuments and ornament from at least volumes VIII and XI (1849 and 1853).[63] The ornament illustrated an article by Ruprich-Robert on the "Cours de composition d'ornement" at the Imperial School of Design, an article in which the vegetable realm is said to furnish "au caprice de l'ornemaniste les ressources les plus fécondes" (fig. 20).[64] Ruskin had no exclusive rights to the use of nature. Nor did Jones alone advocate conventionalization, for Ruprich-Robert says of the flowers illustrated in the plate copied by Van Brunt that

> undoubtedly it will be noted that the plants reproduced in our drawings are not always strictly accurate anatomically. That was precisely our intention. We did not want to render nature faithfully. Monumental art, or the simple caprice of the ornamentalist, demands a certain convention. We have sometimes interpreted our subjects by making them symmetrical.

This is not the place to decide whether Jones profited from Ruprich-Robert's method. Certainly the *Revue* was sufficiently interested in Jones's work to publish, in volume XV (1857), "Des principes essentiels de la composition des ornements," translated from Jones's *Grammar*. Some of the ornament on the Academy seems to reflect a study of Jones, but other ornament, such as that above the Cherry Street entrance (cat. 3-3) or the ironwork of the rear stairway (cat. 3-13), as well as sketchbook drawings for ornament (cat. 3-4), suggest the conventionalization found in the *Revue*. Even in the ornament of this period the duality of Furness and Hewitt's sources is evident.

This ornament was being designed, or executed, while the young Sullivan was in the office, and there can be no doubt that he was deeply affected by Furness's ornamental style. His own early drawings show it. The one he later gave to Frank Lloyd Wright, executed in Paris in November 1874 (about a year after he left Furness), was dependent upon the ornament on the Academy (fig. 21) and may be compared especially with the floral patterns in the tympana of the windows flanking the Broad Street pavilion (cat. 3-2). Sullivan's *System of Architectural Ornament,* finished just before his death in 1924, is a mystical version of Owen Jones. It carries the abstracting principles of floral decoration into an energized, philosophical realm. Furness links Sullivan to Jones (and Ruprich-Robert), and so is a key factor in that progression that led ultimately to the search by Sullivan's own protégé for geometric principles in nature.[65] The result was the totally abstract frieze of Wright's Coonley House of 1908, or the abstract tree that was the basis for the design of the entire Johnson Wax Tower of 1947–50 (fig. 22). Wright's theory of organic architecture was in part an outgrowth of this nineteenth-century process of abstraction from nature.

The spacial organization as well as the decoration of the façade-house of the Academy is characteristic of Furness's mature work. Its stairhall is one of the most impressive spaces in American architecture of any period (cat. 3-9). The decorative combination of incised, floral-patterned walls, arches, and symmetrical, conventionalized ornament found precedent in a church designed by Ruprich-Robert and published in the *Revue* of 1870 (fig. 23). To reach the stairhall the visitor squeezes through a narrow entranceway, itself divided by a trumeau incongruously "supporting" the center of a low segmental arch, into a small foyer, past another divided portal, and so into the stairhall with its brightly lighted stair flowing broadly toward him (cat. 3-8). Emerging from the low, vaulted, relatively dark entry spaces, he suddenly enters the tall, bright, colorful well of space surrounded by grey incised stone or gilt patterned walls, expanded at the upper level through a pointed arcade and lighted from overhead by a metal-framed skylight. This pattern of squeezed entry followed by a radiant open space is a picturesque organization of interior volumes that matches the play of colors and textures on the exterior. It occurs over and over again in Furness's work.[66]

The skylight above the main stairhall is not the only place in the building where iron is visible. In order to provide northern light for studios on the ground floor, Furness rested the north exterior second-floor wall on an exposed iron beam hung from above (cat. 3-7). In the skylighted exhibition spaces exposed iron I-beams are supported on doubled and banded iron columns; or rather, the columns uphold blocky capitals from which fat corbeled fingers extend upward to grasp the beam (cat. 3-12). We need very little to persuade ourselves that Furness and Hewitt followed Viollet-le-Duc in their use of exposed iron here, and that persuasion is found in the pattern of the cast-bronze railing of the main stair (cat. 3-11). That floral pattern is similar, although not identical,

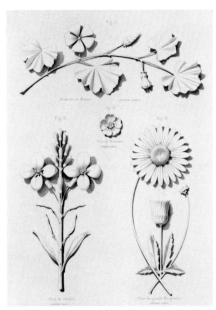

20 Ruprich-Robert. "Cours de composition d'ornement" (from *Revue générale de l'architecture,* XI, 1853, Pl. 20)

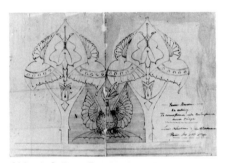

21 Louis Sullivan. Drawing for architectural ornament, November 1874. Avery Architectural Library, Columbia University, New York

22 Frank Lloyd Wright. Johnson Wax Tower, Racine, Wisconsin. 1947–50. Section

65. Here again the full story is more complicated than this outline suggests. There is of course a similar development in Europe at this time.

66. And in the public work of Frank Lloyd Wright. See also note 44.

23 Ruprich-Robert. Interior details of a church (from *Revue,* XXVIII, 1870, Pl. 38)

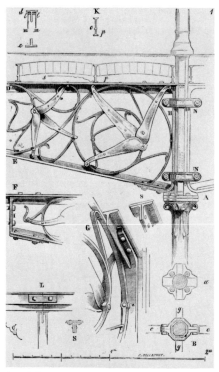

24 E.-E. Viollet-le-Duc. Ornamental ironwork (from *Entretiens,* II, 1872, p. 126)

67. A memorial to Richardson's great-grandfather, designed by Andrews, Jacques and Rantoul of Boston (the first two were associates of Richardson), was installed in Furness's Unitarian Church in 1889.

68. M. G. Van Rensselaer, *Henry Hobson Richardson,* Boston, 1888 (reprint ed., New York, 1969); H.-R. Hitchcock, *The Architecture of H. H. Richardson,* New York, 1936 (rev. ed., 1961; paperback ed., Cambridge, Mass., 1966).

to the ornamental ironwork illustrated in the second volume of the *Entretiens* (fig. 24), published in 1872—the year construction commenced on the Academy. Furness took up Viollet's challenge to produce a stylistically eclectic iron architecture for the nineteenth century.

The *American Architect's* 1876 report on Furness's work (Hewitt, no longer Furness's partner, is not mentioned) said that it was "by far the most important element in the recent building of Philadelphia," although it pronounced the Academy itself a failure because "its lines are 'pestered,' instead of accentuated, by its ornament; and it does not get the benefit of its dimensions." The writer ended by admitting that Furness's work had some Ruskinian virtues, however, for "it is full of life; and the life of it would atone for much worse faults than it shows. It is altogether the most interesting thing, to a student of architecture, to be seen in Philadelphia." Clearly, by the year of the Centennial, Furness had established a fine reputation beyond the confines of his native city.

Designed in 1871 and finished in 1876, the Pennsylvania Academy of the Fine Arts, Furness's first building of national significance, has its counterpart in Boston's Trinity Church, designed in 1872 and finished in 1877, the first work of major significance by another emerging architect, Henry Hobson Richardson (1838–1886). A brief review of Richardson's better known career will help us put Furness's in sharper focus.

Richardson was the great-grandson of Joseph Priestley, the same scientist-divine who had founded the First Unitarian congregation of which Furness's father was pastor.[67] He followed first Horace Howard Furness to Harvard, graduating in 1859, and then R. M. Hunt to the École des Beaux-Arts in Paris, spending the war years there studying, and working for Théodore Labrouste. He returned to the United States following the war, received his first commission (a Unitarian church) in 1866, joined in partnership with Charles Gambrill, formerly of Hunt's atelier, and in June of 1872 won the commission for the design of Trinity Church in Boston. From that date until his untimely death a decade and a half later, Richardson was at the top of the architectural profession in America.[68]

Especially in his early work, Richardson displayed a knowledge of the architecture of both France where he had studied, and England which he visited early and kept up with through publications; but as he matured he came more and more to emulate the Romanesque of France and Spain and the traditional simple granite style of Boston. Eventually he evolved an architecture of massive, bold, colorful but quiet characteristics (fig. 33). The simple, stable horizontality of his work contrasted sharply with the complex, top-heavy verticality of Furness's.

There is no absolute proof that Furness and Richardson ever knew one another, although their paths were tangential so often it is hard to imagine they did not cross. But they certainly knew of one another's work; their careers were coeval; and their personalities and work so different, that the one is the perfect foil for the other. Richardson was gregarious and entertained expansively at his Brookline, Massachusetts, house. He had a keen appreciation of the value of good public relations. Furness grew into a sharp-tongued curmudgeon who sought refuge from his critics either on horseback at his country house, "Idlewild," in Media (fig. 25), or by retreating into the den he built onto his ordinary Philadelphia rowhouse (fig. 26). This was as eclectic as his architecture, a bewildering accumulation of guns, snowshoes, stuffed birds, a ram's head, nature prints, caricatures, Indian blankets, mugs, pipes, and rough-plank furniture that looked as if it were in the wilds of Montana. The author of *Artistic Houses* could only gasp that it was "absolutely unique."[69]

The divergent careers and personalities of these two Victorian architects are summed up in the participation of each in the Philadelphia Centennial Exhibition of 1876. Richardson exhibited several buildings and projects and walked off with an award.[70] Furness designed the gaudy Brazilian Court in the Main Building (cat. 12) but exhibited only some dogs in the dog show and went unpremiated.[71] Richardson's work was the subject of several handsome portfolios during his lifetime, and he received the tribute of a major monograph just two years after his death. He has always been justly considered the most important influence of his day—the force that shifted the direction of American architecture away from the picturesque. Furness's work remained firmly within the bounds of the picturesque as long as he was in full control in the office, and only a renewed interest in picturesque architecture has rediscovered him. Although his work was diametrically opposed to that of Richardson, he was briefly, but significantly, influenced by the example of his contemporary in New England. As we pursue Furness's career we must also keep Richardson's in mind.

While the Academy was in the initial stages of construction, Furness and Hewitt completed the first unit of the Jewish Hospital on Broad Street. The main building (cat. 4-5), finished in 1873, was an asymmetrical fieldstone pile with a high-roofed main pavilion, and polychromatic brick patterns in the arches above openings and in the cornice and dormers that broke up the skyline of the main section. It was not a work of great distinction, and suffered by comparison with Furness's later work at the Hospital.

The Guarantee Trust and Safe Deposit Company building (cat. 6), which stood at 316–320 Chestnut Street until removed in the 1950s by the National Park Service to make way for a sham Georgian structure, was the commercial counterpart of the Academy. It was completed in 1875, but a preliminary study for the façade appears in a sketchbook dated 1873 (cat. 6-1). Like the Academy, this was a long, rectangular building which developed into a monumental front on Chestnut Street, where the twin-towered façade was reminiscent of medieval gateways illustrated by Viollet-le-Duc.[72] The central opening, choked with pedestals, columns, arches and an abstract floral brooch, was squeezed further by the taller corner masses: the pressure on the entrance was immense (cat. 6-2). Again the visitor sensed the need to shoulder his way through the cluttered opening to gain the interior. And again that interior was a tall, open, colorful banking room that must have filled him with a sense of relief (cat. 6-6). Incised floral patterns, richly wrought iron details, colorful patterns of tile—these elements, characteristic of Furness and Hewitt's work, were carried over from the Academy. The decorative ironwork of stair railings, spandrels, and entrance hardware was among the finest of their collaborative work (cat. 6-8, 6-9).

The beleaguered entrance here and elsewhere in Furness's work is one effect of the play of forces he built into his wall surfaces. Many Victorian architects used polychromy as a kind of message-sending device to signal the forces within a wall. Stone lintels in brick walls, exaggerated stone keys and imposts in brick arches, tile belt courses, and so on, all emphasize the real or imagined

25 Frank Furness on horseback, after 1900. Courtesy George Wood Furness

26 Interior of den, Frank Furness house, Philadelphia, before 1883. Courtesy George Wood Furness

69. *Artistic Houses*, 2 vols., New York, 1883, II, p. 169.

70. *International Exhibition, 1876. Official Catalogue. Part II*, Philadelphia, 1876, pp. 32–37; *United States International Exhibition, 1876. Reports and Awards*, VII, Group XXVII, Award 91, p. 57.

71. *Pennsylvania and the Centennial Exposition*, Philadelphia, 1878, II, p. 103. He probably also designed the Gate now on East River Drive for the Centennial. See attributions in the checklist.

72. Viollet-le-Duc, *Entretiens: Atlas*, Paris, 1864, Pls. XXVII, XXXI.

dynamics of the wall structure. Furness caricatured this practice. Here large windows to right and left of the main portal were pinched in at the imposts, then skewed back, as if the huge, blocky, smooth-dressed Ohio stones were being forced by the light brick walls in upon the void created by the arch they are supposed to support (cat. 6-3). Such histrionics were a fundamental part of Furness's architecture.[73]

Of less interest than either of the buildings already discussed, or the work at the Zoological Garden, was the First Troop, Philadelphia City Cavalry Armory of 1874 (cat. 7), although given Furness's military experience, he must have enjoyed the commission. A battlemented, three-story fortress with rusticated stone base and red pressed brick walls with black diaper patterns, only the unrelated scale of the basement and attic windows and those of the second story enlivened this otherwise ordinary design.

The work at the Zoo of 1875–76 (cat. 11) coincided with the breaking up of the firm of Furness and Hewitt into separate entities. Hewitt alone is credited with the Antelope House and the Aviary, Furness with the Elephant House and Restaurant. Although Hewitt is given the gatehouses, too (the only part of their work still standing), Furness must have had a hand in their design. The patchwork stone and elongated eaves brackets reappear in his later work.

Studies for the Elephant House (cat. 11-2) and the Restaurant (cat. 11-8) survive in the sketchbooks. The Elephant House was a long rectangular building providing "a single row of elevated enclosures, a broad walk and retiring rooms for spectators, and ample accommodations for hay," according to the zoological society report of its construction. The exterior, known from woodcut illustrations and photographs (cat. 11-4), was a typical combination of brick walls, rusticated granite base, half-timbered upper story, and high-pitched slate roofs framing a symmetrical, pavilion-ended composition rather like that for the contemporary Shamokin Railroad Station (fig. 34). Pavilions in the form of square towers that expand on brackets as they rise to high-profiled, dormered roofs become one of Furness's favorite picturesque compositional devices, especially in suburban domestic work.

The Restaurant was capped with a brilliantly colored roof and lighted within through colored glass windows under the eaves. On the porch Furness again incorporated the scalloped horseshoe arches he had used at Rodef Shalom (cat. 11-6). His frequent use of these Islamic details in the mid-seventies—they also appear on his Brazilian Pavilion at the Exhibition and the furniture he designed for Horace at this period—perhaps stems from Hunt's cast-iron Tweedy and Co. Store in New York of 1871–72, where similar details enrich the façade (fig. 27). But ultimately they probably derive from the works of Owen Jones.

Furness's services went beyond the architectural shell. He also designed fittings and furnishings, especially during the early part of his career. For the Pennsylvania Academy and elsewhere he created metallic light fixtures in angular floral patterns (cat. 3–10), and all of his ecclesiastical interiors originally contained reading desks, pulpits, pews, and so on, with conventionalized or natural plant-inspired ornament (cat. 24-7). The chairs from Rodef Shalom (cat. 2-3, 2-4) are among the earliest preserved examples of his work, and show

27 Richard M. Hunt. Tweedy and Co. Store, New York. 1871–72 (from *AABN*, I, 1876)

Plate 4 Thomas Hockley House. Exterior detail from west

73. There will be those who will see in this the "sado-masochistic" aspect of associationism discussed by George Hersey, in *Victorian Gothic*, pp. 53 ff.

28 Frank Furness. Desk and chair, designed for Horace Howard Furness. c. 1875. Collection George Wood Furness. Photograph by Cervin Robinson

that from the beginning he was after an electrifying surface effect of lines and shapes. For his domestic furniture, of which some preserved pieces were made for Horace's city and country houses (fig. 28), he relied heavily upon the popular pattern books of the period. Primary among these were Bruce Talbert's *Gothic Forms Applied to Furniture* (1867) and Charles Eastlake's *Hints on Household Taste* (1868). But here, too, he found parallels in French sources, such as the ecclesiastical furniture illustrated in the *Revue* (fig. 23). From these sources he derived the basic structural lines of his furniture, which he then filled in with his own incised floral or animal patterns.[74] This furniture was as eclectically designed as his architecture, to which it is closely related. Horace's bookcases and desk, for example, display the scalloped horseshoe arches of contemporary buildings such as the Zoo Restaurant. Mantels and woodwork within the buildings formed transitional elements between the architecture and the furniture.

## 7. Furness "Alone" (1875–81)

Furness practiced without a partner for a number of years after Hewitt's departure. Of course he was not entirely alone. Among other assistants, Allen Evans, who became his full partner in 1881, was in the office from the beginning of the seventies.[75]

In this period the more overt aspects of Victorian Gothic influence, the "pantalettes" to quote Sullivan, begin to assume a less important role in his work, although they never entirely disappear. With Hewitt gone, Furness could depend more upon his own sources: his French-oriented training and the work of his mentor, Richard Morris Hunt. During this period he carried on the development of the design of the small city bank, created a number of important civic commissions, and began to work for the railroads. In short, his practice had become substantial and varied and his creative powers were at their height. For the next twenty years, Furness went from strength to strength.

The evolution of Furness's mature style in the seventies can be traced in the series of banks for small urban lots, either at the corner or in the middle of the block: the Philadelphia Warehouse Company of 1872–73 (by Furness and Hewitt); the Centennial National Bank of 1876; the first unit of the Provident Life and Trust Company of 1876–79, a masterpiece that stood at 409 Chestnut until pulled down just over a decade ago to make way for a parking lot; and the Kensington National Bank of 1877. As a design problem the bank resolved itself into two parts: the façade, for which there are a series of studies in the sketchbooks (cat. 6-1 and 13-3), and the banking room. In these works Furness broke with the twin-towered formula of the Guarantee, and moved from Hewitt's Anglophilia toward his own sources. In the process he created a very personal style.

The corner building for the Philadelphia Warehouse Company (cat. 5) reused much of the vocabulary of the Pennsylvania Academy and the Guarantee: rusticated base, dressed stone and brick walls, striped voussoirs forming round intrados and pointed extrados, and a crenelated skyline. The entrance was on the bevel between squat, banded columns supporting a small balcony with a patterned iron railing. Floral ornament lurked in corners and crevices.

The Centennial Bank is also a corner building with entrance on the bevel (cat. 13). It is red brick Gothic, but it is not totally dependent upon English

74. I am indebted to Mrs. Elizabeth Sussman for sharing her knowledge of nineteenth-century furniture with me.

75. See note 90.

precedent. The façade was probably developed with knowledge of the design of a Boston town house by Ware and Van Brunt published in César Daly's *Revue* for 1870 (fig. 29). In the center of the town house façade is a narrow polygonal bay resting on a single column.[76] The central windows stack up four stories to include the dormer in a mansard roof. Only at the second and third levels are these central windows flanked by other windows in the beveled sides, and these are capped by a hip roof interrupted by the central stack. The authorship of this town house and its publication in the *Revue* make it very likely that Furness knew this design. He used this intersection of projecting bay and hip roof on the Centennial and Provident banks, although he significantly altered the proportions.

At the Centennial Bank Furness used a deep orange-red pressed brick on the exterior. Contrasting colors are held to a minimum, and contrasting materials follow the brick closely in color; but this does not mean that this is a passive design. As at the Guarantee, we hasten through a beleaguered entrance lost between the massive squat columns[77] of the central salient, itself squeezed into an elongated, gabled bay bristling with caricatured crockets and flanked by an incipient shed with slate roof and pinch-topped windows (cat. 13-2). The dramatic effect of this exterior is achieved by this sense of pressure, of converging forces, and of confrontation between the overscaled, uncarved blocks and stubby columns flanking the pinched entry and the small-scale decorative elements achieved by the simple manipulation of bricks. The main cornice, for example, builds the two- and three-dimensional cubical units of red and black bricks into an abstract composition worthy of the early twentieth century (cat. 13-1).

The *American Architect* noted that "in a sort of crocketed gable [over the main entrance of the Centennial Bank], the tympanum of the arch [is] decorated with the same . . . brilliant glass tiles, sparkling with gold and color, which were used in the front of the Academy of the Fine Arts."[78] We can add that these same tiles were a marked feature of Furness's Brazilian Court in the Main Building of the Centennial Exhibition itself (cat. 12). This structure was destroyed long ago, but it is known from old views and from a description in the *American Architect.*[79] The Brazilian Court, like the contemporary Zoo Restaurant (cat. 11-6), was surrounded by a long rectangular screen of Islamic arches that led to an entrance pavilion opened by a huge scalloped arch and capped with a high hip roof. In form it was not unlike the whole of the Academy, and the decorative floral merlons surmounting the screens and pavilion were identical to those on the central pavilion of the Academy (plate 3). But a more important link between these two designs and the Centennial Bank was the use of the bright patterns in glass still to be seen on the surviving works. Apparently in the mid-seventies Furness was interested in achieving rich, permanent color patterns of floral ornament, and so, according to the *American Architect,* he invented a kind of glass tile painted on the back with "various designs in rich transparent colors" behind which he placed a layer of gold foil and a layer of tin foil to hold the gold. "The gold-foil imparts to the colors . . . a peculiarly beautiful lustre. Thus, for instance, the green will be a good imitation of the green on a beetle's wing. . . ." The rich, metallic effect of these glass tiles can still be seen on the Academy and the Centennial Bank, but Furness apparently did not use them again (he switched to the leaded white-glass designs found in the Griscom House and elsewhere). This search for permanent, bright, vitreous coloring in architecture was characteristic of the mid-

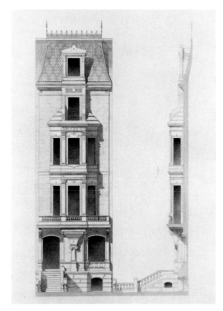

29 Ware and Van Brunt. Town House for Beacon Street, Boston. 1864 (from *Revue*, XXVIII, 1870, Pl. 60)

76. The house was erected at 117 Beacon Street in 1864. See Bainbridge Bunting, *Houses of Boston's Back Bay,* Cambridge, Mass., 1967, pp. 125–127, 403.

77. Stubby columns are certainly a Furness hallmark, but like many other features in his work which at first seem so personal, they have their origin and parallel in the works of others. For example, they occur in Richardson's work as early as 1869 (Agawam National Bank, Springfield, Mass.) and as late as 1879 (Town Hall, North Easton, Mass.). Their appearance in the Delano House of 1875 in Barrytown, N.Y., the work of the Anglophile John Sturgis, strongly suggests, as Margaret Floyd reminds me, that they have English precedents. But it should be reemphasized here that it is not *what* derivative features Furness used that make his work exceptional, but *how* he used them.

78. *AABN*, I, December 23, 1876, p. 414.

79. *AABN*, I, May 13, 1876, p. 160.

30 Addison Hutton. The Provident Life and Trust Company, Philadelphia. 1872 (from J. D. McCabe, *Illustrated History of the Centennial Exhibition*, 1876)

seventies. During these same years John LaFarge and Louis Tiffany began their own experiments with opalescent and lustre glass, experiments that led eventually to the brilliant decorative windows and objects of art that brightened domestic and other interiors in the 1880s and after.[80] And these were frequently cast in floral patterns.[81]

In the Centennial Bank Furness developed his own expressive vocabulary, his own blend of sources, to produce within the general Victorian style personal work of great distinction. At the Provident he took the final step.

The Provident (cat. 14) was Furness's own version of the standard, centralized, three-bay façade pattern that marked Addison Hutton's earlier building for the firm on Fourth Street (fig. 30), as well as James Windrim's just-finished Bank of Pennsylvania on the adjacent lot on the west of Furness's site. The Windrim and Furness banks formed part of "Bankers' Row," a series of banking houses that stretched (and, with the exception of Furness's building, still stretches) along the north side of Chestnut Street between Fourth and Fifth streets (fig. 31). The contrast between Hutton's routine façade and Furness's arresting one is the measure of Furness's personal style.

Furness's Provident stood out among his own works too. The central salient, corbeled out over the entrance and pierced with a pointed arch, the intersecting shed roof, and the stubby columns flanking the entrance—all are taken over from the Centennial Bank. The contrasting stonework would be used again on the Kensington, but the effect at the Provident was unlike any of the others. The stone, of two distinct colors and textures, was used in massive blocks that called forth huge ornamental detail, such as the gargantuan leaves that sprouted from the top of the shed to either side of the corbeled central bay (cat. 14-2). The pressures Furness introduced here make those of his earlier buildings seem weak. Overweight details come together with a violent crunch we now associate with the pro football field. Masses of stone pressed down over the entrance, forcing the columns into stumps. The segmental arch above the entry struggled against the rest of the façade to maintain a passage into the interior. The visitor rushed beneath the overhanging cliffs of chunky masonry . . . and emerged into a characteristically top-lighted, rectangular, single volume of space with high walls of green and white Minton tiles, rising straight up to polychrome iron girders (cat. 14-7). These were ornamented with punched, abstract, geometric patterns that looked like the starting point for those elaborate floral designs that Louis Sullivan later published in his *System.*

An appreciative and perceptive writer for the *Philadelphia Evening Telegraph,* who reported that the rising façade of the Provident had put a "constant strain on the public mind," astutely characterized this work by saying that Furness's strong point "seems to have been to get all his decorative detail large enough

80. There is an English parallel in the work of William DeMorgan, who was experimenting with lustreware in the mid-seventies.

81. LaFarge's decorative work is the subject of a recent dissertation: H. B. K. Weinberg, "The Decorative Work of John LaFarge," Columbia University, 1972. For examples of LaFarge and Tiffany floral-pattern glass from the late seventies, see R. J. Clark, *The Arts and Crafts Movement in America 1876–1916,* Princeton, 1972, pp. 18–19.

31 "Bankers' Row" (from *The Baxter Panoramic Business Directory,* May 1879)

for a building about double the size of the one he puts it on, so that it is apt to have a decidedly awkward appearance. [Here] he appears to have succeeded in getting his detail larger and more out of proportion than ever."[82] The writer thought he understood Furness's motive, too, and began his article with the description of a cartoon in *Punch* representing two men, one tall and hand-some, one small with distorted features. By pushing up his nose with his cane tip, the shorter of the two calls attention to his own sorry features and draws away "from his handsome companion some of the attention and notice which the latter usually has all to himself." Thus Furness planted an eye-catcher in the staid row of banks in order to draw attention to the Provident.

What our advertising experts do now with neon tubing, Furness achieved through caricature, putting fully developed architectural details onto a stunted field—just as he drew in one of his sketchbooks a caricature with fully developed head on a miniature body. Like the grotesque in *Punch,* this dwarfish figure calls attention to himself by standing on tiptoe and raising an arm over his head in order to be SOO BIG (fig. 12). The accompanying inscription asks the kind of question that (to quote the *Telegraph* on the Provident once again) "puzzled the mind of the average citizen with anxiety": IS IT A NIGHTMARE OR ONLY A CRAMP? The dilemma keeps the object in the public eye. Unfortunately, by the late 1950s the Quaker owners of the bank had decided that the Provident was both a nightmare and a cramp, and tore down the building. It came as no surprise. Furness's father had warned what would happen to the uncommon in Philadelphia.

This first unit of the Provident is without doubt Furness's masterpiece at a small scale. Although the design evolved out of English and French sources, no specific precedents outside of Furness's own past can be itemized here. This was a personal building, yet thoroughly American too. It was as irreverent and exaggerated as the contemporary humor of Mark Twain. The Provident represented the culmination of the development of Furness's genius well before his fortieth year.

In comparison, the Kensington Bank is anticlimactic, although it is of interest here as one of the purest Néo-Grec works Furness ever designed (cat. 15-1). The building follows the corner form of the Philadelphia Warehouse and the Centennial and the stonework of the Provident. The entrance, again at the bevel, is beneath a balcony supported by chunky corbels and enclosed by a row of fat balusters set between massive blocks. Furness used dressed and rock-faced granite in two shades of grey to create a rectangular composition in shallow layers. The surfaces are enriched with incised linear and floral ornament, ironwork grills of abstract patterns at the windows, and roundels and other Néo-Grec details (cat. 15-3). There was little here to recall Furness's association with Hewitt.

Behind the façade of the Kensington Bank was an impressive vessel of space, characteristically colorful, metallic, and top-lighted. The *American Architect* described the ceiling as "dome-shaped, entirely of iron, supporting a large skylight. The iron panels . . . will be picked out in gold and colors." It paralleled the rich interiors of all Furness's banks.

The primary reliance upon the expressive qualities of manipulated red pressed brick patterns and surfaces, combined with plastic handling of details, walls, and masses that marks the Centennial Bank, marked several other works of

82. *Philadelphia Evening Telegraph,* October 3, 1878, quoted in James C. Massey, "The Provident Trust Buildings," *JSAH,* XIX, May 1960, pp. 79–80.

Plate 5 William H. Rhawn House: "Knowlton." Exterior from south

Plate 6 William H. Rhawn House: "Knowlton." Stairhall

this period as well. Although these designs begin before the break with Hewitt, they can be taken as among the most characteristic of Furness's works: the Hockley House (cat. 9), Jefferson Medical College (cat. 10), and the addition to the Deaf and Dumb Asylum (cat. 8), all between 1874 and 1877. The Library Company (cat. 17) of 1878–80 is related to these, yet is even richer. In these works the coloration may be even, but surface contrasts of texture and highlight and shadow combine with rich and varied silhouettes created by the multiplication of gables, ridges, dormers and—Furness's hallmark—chimneys (cat. 8-1). These are masterful, abstract, top-heavy, cubical compositions in brick, rivaled only perhaps by those of his Spanish near-contemporary, Antonio Gaudí, in Barcelona. These buildings are without the overt formal challenges of the Provident. Furness developed here a colorful, variable, and relatively discrete treatment of brick forms and surfaces over workable plans that was copied all over the city in the seventies and eighties by speculative builders. A walk down almost any street in West Philadelphia, and especially the Powelton-Mantua section, will reveal row upon row of houses turned out from this formula. Unfortunately these houses, like Furness's own buildings, are now disappearing one after the other.[83]

Of this group only the addition to the Deaf and Dumb Asylum (now Philadelphia College of Art) and the Hockley House remain. Besides the rich brickwork of the exterior (plate 4) and the vast stairhall in the interior, the most striking aspect of the Hockley House is the oversized and formalized floral ornament in the stone tympanum of the entrance porch (cat. 9-2)—a piece of angular design related to the ornament of the Academy (cat. 3-2). The Jefferson Medical College Hospital formed an L-shaped five-story block with a skylighted room filling in the angle (cat. 10-1). It was a straightforward scheme enriched on the exterior by patterned brick belt courses joining the tops of the windows, dormers, and chimneys. The main stack grew out of the wall on corbels at the third-floor level, then split in two as it rose around a window in the fifth floor. This split-flue chimney was a device Furness used throughout his career. It appears, for example, in the parish house of the First Unitarian Church of the mid-eighties (cat. 24-8), and in the Jayne House of the mid-nineties (cat. 37-3). Although its ultimate origin was probably English, Furness undoubtedly picked up this penetrated chimney from Hunt, who had designed such a fireplace for the interior of the Griswold House at Newport.[84]

The façade of the Library Company (cat. 17-1), as George Tatum has already observed, was a "Victorianization" of the Federal style library designed a century earlier by William Thornton.[85] With rusticated stone base, stone imposts and keys, and ornamental detail, all harking back to the original building, the Library Company was externally the most elaborate of this group of brick buildings. The interior was a series of book-lined rooms, skylighted and galleried, with structural metal exposed as mill-shaped I-beams and banded columns (cat. 17-2). Such an arrangement was not as significant in the development of library design in this country as the iron-and-glass book stack Furness was to use at the University Library ten years later; however, these rooms were characteristic not only of Furness's interiors but of many libraries of the middle of the century. This interior, in fact, follows a type that is best known from Hunt's Lenox Library in New York (1870–75), published the year before Furness began the Library Company.[86]

The Church of the Redeemer for Seamen and Their Families of 1878 still stands in a residential area in South Philadelphia (cat. 16). A comparison

83. Furness's brick style of the 1870s paralleled the contemporary "panel brick style" of Ware and Van Brunt and others in Boston. See Bunting, *Back Bay*, pp. 157–158, 188–194. Both certainly derive from the exterior of Hunt's Tenth Street Studio Building.

84. I owe this information to Thomas M. Slade. Margaret Floyd tells me that English antecedents can be found, expecially in the work of Charles Barry, and that John Sturgis's Barstow House of 1862, at Portsmouth near Newport, has a split-flue fireplace with window above. Furness's use of this form was not exclusive.

85. Tatum, *Penn's Great Town*, p. 111; cf. *Philadelphia Public Ledger*, February 20, 1879, p. 3.

86. *AABN*, II, September 1, 1877, p. 280.

with the Library Company (which was on the drafting board at the same time) demonstrates the range of expressive means at Furness's disposal at the height of his career. The exterior of the Seamen's Church—actually the half of the building to the west was a school—looks like the advertising display of a jocular mason. The front of the school (cat. 16-6, left) is divided into rectangular panels above the ground floor of "crazy quilt," random rubble masonry that Furness and Evans used again at the Undine Barge Club building on the Schuylkill River in 1882–83.[87] The timberwork above is filled in with brick laid in diaper, soldier, and basket-weave patterns. The entrance to the school is beneath a corbeled bay of random ashlar that extends down the left door jamb but not the right! This entrance bay is capped with a jerkinheaded, open gable the deep overhang of which is supported by double, turned stickwork brackets. The main gable of the church itself has an inset pointed arch of wood supported by even more elaborate laminated and turned brackets (cat. 16-7). This combination of brick, stone, and openwork in wood, plus the juxtapositioning of arched gables, hip roofs, jerkinheads, and sheds, are features common in Furness's domestic architecture of the period. They are also common features of Hunt's Queen Anne domestic work, and frequently occurred in illustrations to the American Architect after its founding in 1876 (fig. 32).[88]

The plan of the Seamen's Church is uncomplicated (cat. 16-2). The school has a central corridor leading back to a rear, double dogleg stair. The church is a broad, stubby space, covered with an open gable (cat. 16-3) supported by arched timbers in turn resting upon side trusses which span the length of the nave between corner supports (cat. 16-4, 16-5). The effect is of an unbraced hammerbeam roof.

The glass clerestory windows here, which admit polychromatic light to play among the roof timbers, are repeated in the second-story locker room of the Undine Barge Club (cat. 23-8). The roof of this locker room is supported by timberwork marked on the exterior by what appear to be decorative wood pendants hanging from the clerestory windows. Straight, thin, and regularly spaced, they contrast with the patchwork, undressed brownstone wall and the varied, towered, and galleried exterior massing of the building as a whole (cat. 23-1). The brick chimney stack on the west side, its plantlike stem rising from long slender roots to a flowering top (plate 7), composes with the rubble wall, the wood balcony supported by diagonal braces, and the double eaves gutters to produce one of the most memorable vignettes in nineteenth-century American architecture.

## 8. Furness and Evans (1881–c. 1895)

In 1871 Furness received a letter from a woman in Paoli asking him to employ her nephew Allen Evans (1845–1925), then a draftsman in the office of the venerable Samuel Sloan. Furness replied that Evans would have to unlearn everything Sloan had taught him, but "if Mr. Evans can spare the time, it would be of benefit to him to work with Mr. Hewitt and myself."[89] Evans did join the pair, and became Furness's partner in 1881. When Louis C. Baker and E. J. Dallett assumed interests in the firm in 1885 it became Furness, Evans and Company. It retained that name, despite an increasing number of silent partners, until well after Furness's death in 1912.[90]

Evans's portrait in the Merion Cricket Club, of which he was a founder, officer, and eventually president (1907–13), shows him holding a cricket bat rather than the architect's T-square and triangle. Clubby and affable, he appears

87. An instructive measure of the polar styles of Furness and Richardson can be made by comparing this random rubble stonework with the neat ashlar of the contemporary Crane Memorial Library at Quincy, Mass.

88. See note 91.

89. William Campbell, "Frank Furness," Architectural Review, CX, November 1951, p. 312.

90. A list of employees and associates of Furness includes the following. 1867–71: Fraser and George Hewitt. 1871–75: William M. Camac, Allen Evans, George and William Hewitt, Louis H. Sullivan. 1876–81: Evans, Camac, W. Neilson Clark, Edward Hazelhurst, Henry Pettit, and Frank Price. 1881–85: Evans, Camac, Louis C. Baker, E. James Dallett, James Fassitt, and John Stewardson. After 1885: Evans, Baker, Camac, Dallett, Fassitt, Morgan Bunting, George W. Casey, Joseph Dingee, Walter Furness, George Howe, Joseph Huston, Herman Kleinfelter, Louis F. Marie, Maximillian Nirdlinger, Joseph Sims, and Charles Willing.

32 Richard M. Hunt. Appleton House, Newport, Rhode Island. 1875 (from *AABN*, I, 1876)

to have been sufficiently self-effacing professionally to get along with his explosive partner, but there is no evidence that he was a gifted designer. Even when clients specified—as happened in later years—that Evans, not Furness, design their buildings, evidence indicates that Furness took a hand in the work. Evans's social position gave the firm an aura of respectability it could never have achieved had Furness alone been in command, though the latter continued to steer its architectural course.

The high achievement of the 1870s continued through the 1880s as building after building rose from the Philadelphia pavement, much to the perplexity and even chagrin of the Philadelphia public. Not all the aggressive design can be assigned to Furness, however, for the Victorian city housed other architects of unrestricted imagination, men such as Willis G. Hale, Davis Edmund Supplee, and Theophilus Parsons Chandler. By the end of the century they had filled Philadelphia with more of what the *Architectural Record* labeled "architectural aberrations" than any other city in America. But in the end convention and complacency have carried the day. Few of their works have survived the reshaping of Philadelphia in the post–World War II era.

Furness's work for the major business and banking firms and railroad companies of Philadelphia led to commissions by some of their executives—such as Alexander Cassatt, president of the Pennsylvania Railroad, or the banker William H. Rhawn—for suburban domestic designs. The variety of this suburban work can be exemplified by a series of four houses largely of the 1880s: the Rhawn House of 1879–81, the Griscom House of 1881 and later, the Shipley House of 1882, and the Winsor House of 1887. The last three were additions to existing structures.

"Knowlton," the Rhawn House (cat. 18), looks like a huge slate tent from the entrance to the estate. A sheltering roof dominates the western view. As usual Furness evolved a rich composition over a relatively simple plan (cat. 18-4, 18-5). Here this is basically a double-barred T or patriarchal cross (☦) with, reading from right to left, four-story upper bar, three-story lower bar, and two-story stem surrounded by a one-story porch. The broad triangular roof begins at the eaves line of the porch (cat. 18-1), flows upward past shed dormers to the roof cresting, broadens to include the lower bar, then rises to the roof cresting and brick chimneys above the upper bar. On the east the exterior falls straight back to ground line (cat. 18-3).

The exterior walls are of fieldstone, slate, and framed clapboards (plate 5). The sheds, arched gables, and jerkinheaded dormers that jab at the sky, the rectangular framing of the wood bay, and the bracketed balcony are all common features of the domestic Queen Anne. They are found on other work of this period by Furness, such as the Seamen's Church, and mark the contemporary Newport houses of Richard Morris Hunt as well (fig. 32).[91]

The house is entered from the porch through a passage into the central stairhall that occupies the lower bar of the plan (plate 6). To the right the parallel upper bar contains sitting room, dining room, pantry, and serving rooms (a later addition). The kitchen is still in the basement. A polygonal bay off the dining room marks one end of the stem of the patriarchal cross (cat. 18-9); the fireplace in the parlor occupies the other. The house is very well preserved; although it lacks the original decoration and color on walls and ceilings, it retains the stained glass, light fixtures, tiles, and woodwork. The paneling of the entry (cat. 18-10), which to our eyes seems prophetic of De

91. Two cottages by Eidlitz at Englewood, N. J., should be recalled here. Erected about 1860 according to Montgomery Schuyler, and hence earlier than Hunt's Griswold House at Newport, their exposed stickwork frames and scalloped horseshoe arches recur frequently in the work of both Hunt and Furness. Photographs of these cottages accompany Schuyler's article on Eidlitz in the *Architectural Record*, XXIV, September 1908, pp. 164–179, but not in the edition of Schuyler's writings cited in note 28.

Stijl composition, most certainly derives from patterns of Japanese wood design that Furness might have seen at the Centennial Exhibition or in the *American Architect* or other publications. The mantelpieces that ornament the main rooms and the bedrooms (cat. 18-12, 18-13) are derived from the publications of Charles Eastlake.

The history of the poorly preserved Griscom House is as complex as its exterior design (cat. 20). The older house, remodeled by Furness, is the block to the left rear of the huge main house, added by Furness in two stages. The incredibly fragmented exterior of the addition—a plastic chorus of towers, bays, sheds, gables, and chimneys (cat. 20-1)—was further complicated by patterns of fieldstone and (originally) shingles in a fish-scale pattern. When moving shadows of the shade trees fall on these surfaces, the house dissolves into total incomprehensibility. The dramatic effect of the front is made more piquant by a taunting suggestion of a symmetry that is not present. The block is an eroded square C with recessed center and corner pavilions. In the recess the main dormer and second-story bay suggest a central axis, but the entrance porch is off-center and there is no balanced development to either side. There is just the hint that one might have been arranged.

The gabled entry gives access to one side of the central hall (cat. 20-4), containing a Jacobean fireplace and a stairway to the upper level visible through a galleried well. Sitting room, dining room, library, and parlor surround the hall.

Throughout this house, the Rhawn House, the University Library, and elsewhere in Furness's work, there are windows of clear or milky glass, with floral motifs indicated by the lead patterning and by variations of glass texture (cat. 20-5). These floral patterns are still highly stylized, but the Griscom House also contains examples of cast and carved ornament rendered very naturalistically. Furness began to combine natural with abstract foliage in the early eighties, but the library, bedroom, and parlor fireplaces here may date from the second enlargement of the house, in 1894. The bedroom fireplace, for example, with its squared circular opening and lush natural vegetation (cat. 20-2), certainly should be dated close to the University Library, and the lilies on the consoles of the library mantel reflect drawings of lilies found in the sketchbooks of the mid-nineties.

The corbeled tower to the left of the main block of the Griscom House is a feature we have seen before in Furness's work, at the Elephant House (cat. 11-1). It appeared again as the water tower at "Winden," the Shipley House, in West Chester (cat. 22-1).

"Winden" was a mid-century gabled fieldstone Italianate box with kitchen ell and ample porch commanding the surrounding landscape from its ridgetop location (cat. 22-2). In remodeling, Furness radiated from this core a library wing (cat. 22-3), a carriage porch with bedroom above (cat. 22-7), and bedrooms over the ell (cat. 22-6). He also provided the central block with a monumental wooden staircase to the third floor, but otherwise left the original classicizing detail untouched wherever possible. The result is a remarkably coherent cruciform house of stone and wood that is in plan not unlike some of the work of the Prairie School architects two decades later.

The additions are in Chalet or Stick Style with details, such as the rectangular paneling of the exterior, much like those at "Knowlton." Other than the characteristically top-heavy water tower, the most arresting detail occurs on the exterior of the wing above the ell (cat. 22-6). The upper floor is cantilevered beyond the lower stone walls on exposed wooden beams. The chimney stack at the end of the wing serves two angled fireplaces in second-floor bedrooms (cat. 22-5). With characteristically irrational humor Furness made it appear as if this brick stack rests upon a thin sheet of slate supported by iron rails. Such a delicate support for a visually heavy load is used elsewhere in Furness's work, most notably ten years later at the University Library.

At the Winsor House the original structure was enriched vertically by patterned brick gables, dormers, and chimneys, and horizontally by the addition of a dining room and kitchen (cat. 28-3, 28-4). Within the original building Furness installed a staircase of latticework oak (cat. 28-1) similar to that at the Griscom House and, opposite, an overscaled red sandstone fireplace (cat. 28-8) of a type he was using in more monumental contemporary buildings such as the Philadelphia B & O Station. The iron firebacks in this house are cast in characteristic lily and sunflower patterns (cat. 28-6, 28-7).

Nothing of great significance survives of the small business buildings erected from Furness's designs in the early eighties. The Penn National Bank of 1882–84 (cat. 21) and the National Bank of the Republic of 1883–84 (cat. 25) were among the more serious losses. The Penn National was developed out of the design for the Kensington Bank of five years earlier. Both were corner banks, although here the entrance was beneath a corner porch rather than on the bevel (cat. 21-2). The main doors in wood, with rectangular panels interrupted by diagonal slashes, sharply contrasted with the delicate iron grills in the pinch-topped lower windows. Interlocking Néo-Grec ornamental forms covered an exterior the main features of which were gawky Palladian windows rising into high gables. The stilted arches of these windows were characteristic of Furness's attenuation of inherited details. So was the high-waisted wall, of continuous smooth squared ashlar masonry rising from the ground to the top of the second floor to culminate in a machicolated belt course that doubled as the impost for the stilted arches. Above this the stonework was rough where it peeked out between the oversized gables enclosing exaggerated voussoirs and rosette studding. At the Penn National Furness personalized Néo-Grec forms he had previously employed with little variation at the Kensington.

The interior, so puzzling from outside, was a characteristic single volume of space with walls rising straight up to a stenciled cove and skylighted ceiling (cat. 21-1). An ornamental iron gallery ran around the space at the level of the Palladian windows, and in the rear the room was divided into two levels, with glazed offices resting upon an exposed iron box-girder punctuated with rosettes. Although we have lost every banking room Furness ever designed, we are fortunate that an image of this space is "preserved" for us in an excellent photograph. It is a small compensation.

In Furness's hands animation could be achieved by relatively quiet means, as at the Penn National Bank, or by bombast, as at the National Bank of the Republic. At the National Bank Furness returned to a more plastic treatment and undoubtedly created the most bewildering of his small commercial buildings (cat. 25-1). Erected in the financial district (cat. 25-2), where many of his other banks were located (not one survives in the area), this culminating work abandoned entirely the Néo-Grec details and the symmetrical façade. Instead Furness split the façade in two and handled each half independently.

The entrance to this mid-block building was to the left. Above it a turret thrust skyward to terminate in a tall candle-snuffer. The divided, arched window to the right supported a chunky dormer. There was no continuous horizontal alignment. Dressed stone, brick, and terra-cotta further enlivened this bedlam of heterogeneous parts. In fact the façade looked as if Furness had glued together pieces from several different, and much larger, buildings in an eclectic rage. Despite the differences in organization and materials, the same can be said about this façade as about that for the Provident of seven years earlier: large-scale architectural features are jammed haphazardly into a very small space, generating pressures that seem about to burst the confines of the party walls. Nothing is static, least of all the incredible half-arch, the work of a man determined to force his work upon the spectator. The public's reaction to the design is unknown; but at least one other architect, C. S. McNally, admired it enough to produce a near copy of the façade as far away as Salem, Oregon, where he was commissioned in 1892 to design the Capital National Bank.[92]

As we have come to expect, the interior contained a huge, skylighted banking room punctuated with a chimneypiece as arresting as the façade (cat. 25-3). It was typical of Furness's fireplaces: a conglomerate "building" in itself, a mass of rough stone and brick, imbricated surfaces, and brilliantly designed and executed floral ornament (cat. 25-4). This chimneypiece is surpassed in Furness's work only by the larger ones in the B & O Station and the reading room of the University Library.

One commercial structure that does exist is the J. T. Bailey and Company building that stretches northward along the east side of Water Street from the corner of Otsego in South Philadelphia (cat. 36). It was built in several sections, perhaps not all by Furness, in the 1880s and 1890s. The brick façade is punctuated by brick or rough-stone arches with smooth skewbacks (cat. 36-1). Although the pattern of fenestration varies from section to section, the regularly spaced pilaster strips give continuity to this overlong elevation; and the top-heavy tower that once rose two stories higher than the rest of the building, above the rough-faced coursed ashlar archway set into the central section, provided a focal point for the whole (cat. 36-3). The most interesting decorative features are the pilaster caps formed of triglyphs beneath roundels, common Néo-Grec details found over and over again in the plates of the *Revue* and elsewhere. Such Néo-Grec touches turn the Bailey façade into a Francophile version of the kind of pilastered brick elevations developed in Philadelphia in the 1850s by Hoxie, Button, and others.[93]

Furness's ecclesiastical work continued through this period. His father had been pastor of the First Unitarian Church long enough to see the building designed by Strickland become crowded and stylistically outmoded. And even though Dr. Furness had retired eight years before his son was commissioned to design the new church at Chestnut and Van Pelt, as pastor emeritus he still had much influence in church affairs. The new building was designed in 1883 and dedicated early in 1886 (cat. 24). Although it is still standing, it has been roughly handled by subsequent alterations. First, the elephantine corner "gazebo," with its high-peaked roof, massive details, and stubby rusticated columns which seemed to collapse like accordions beneath the crushing load, was removed long ago (cat. 24-2). Then, the rock-faced stonework of the exterior has been largely polished smooth. Finally, the ridge openings that

92. Lee Nelson, "White, Furness, McNally and the Capital National Bank of Salem, Oregon," *JSAH*, XIX, May 1960, pp. 57 ff.
93. Winston Weisman, "Philadelphia Functionalism," *JSAH*, XX, March 1961, pp. 3 ff.

sent light down into the interior through the timber roof trusses have been closed (cat. 24-1). Taken together, these changes have considerably weakened Furness's design.

In its present condition the church is a rather simple gable-roofed building fronted by a porch on Chestnut Street decorated with unexceptional fern ornament (cat. 24-4). The main elements of the gable end are the rose window and the aedicule above, an expanded version of the one on Rodef Shalom (cat. 2-2). In the interior, too, Furness made good use of details worked out in earlier ecclesiastical designs, including the synagogue and the Seamen's Church. The plan (cat. 24-3) is cruciform with short transepts bisecting the broad nave. The roof is supported by delicate trusses of iron rods and light wood timbers. With the original patterns of light filtering down from the ridge, this must have been one of the most impressive small-scale ecclesiastical spaces in Victorian America.

An arched chapel, rather like that in the later Williamson School (cat. 30-3), was originally the main feature of the parish house. Both chapels have since been altered, but that at the parish house retains at one end a brick fireplace with naturalistic carved-stone flowers enlivening the sill of a window deep-set above the fire opening (cat. 24-10). Furness created this unexpected void by separating the fireplace flues. The effect is startling. Flanking windows create a sea of bright illumination in which the penetrated brick mass floats freely.

Churches and banks did not occupy all of Furness's time. From the mid-seventies on the railways were among his most important clients. The urbanization of the United States following the Civil War saw the creation of dense commercial civic cores surrounded by outlying domestic suburbs. Before the motor car these centers of daily life were connected by the railroad, and this gave rise to a new building type. The small commuter depot joined the large terminal as a hub of the railway age. The architect of such a depot had two tasks: provide transient shelter and mark that shelter as a transportation node. Edward Lamson Henry's *The 9:45 Accommodation,* of 1867 (Metropolitan Museum of Art, New York), depicts the wayside depot as the center of suburban activity. Its wood Gothic station characterized railway architecture at the beginning of the careers of two men who were to design some of the finest postwar buildings of the type.

In a series of commuter stations on the railway lines leading out from Boston, H. H. Richardson in his last five years developed a design of spreading proportions with horizontal hip roof projecting as shelter far beyond exterior walls of granite ashlar. They were rich in color and in patterns of highlight and shadow. Of the few that remain, the Old Colony Station at North Easton, Massachusetts, of 1881 shows the taut outline and ground-hugging proportions of the type (fig. 33).

Richardson designed not only depots but railway cars for the Boston and Albany Railroad, and he reputedly wanted to design grain elevators and steamboats; for these desires and achievements he was said by Lewis Mumford to have been "the first architect in America who was ready to face the totality of modern life."[94] Furness did design interiors of ferryboats as well as railway cars, and his work for the railroads not only began earlier than Richardson's

33 H. H. Richardson. Old Colony Railroad Station, North Easton, Massachusetts. 1881. Photograph by Jean Baer O'Gorman

Plate 7 Undine Barge Club. Exterior detail from west

94. Lewis Mumford, *The Brown Decades*, New York, 1955, p. 118.

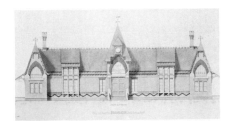

34 Frank Furness. Philadelphia and Railroad Depot, Shamokin, Pennsylvania. 1876. Drawing. Collection Mr. and Mrs. Alfred W. Hesse, Jr., Gladwyne

35 E.-E. Viollet-le-Duc. "Hôtel de Ville (Emploi du fer)" (from *Entretiens: Atlas*, 1864, Pl. XXIV)

but included some major terminals as well. Here as elsewhere the largeness of Richardson's historical shadow has obscured the achievements of his contemporaries.

An indication of Furness's extensive work for the railroads is contained in a letter he wrote to John E. Wooten, general manager of the Philadelphia and Reading Railroad Company, dated December 23, 1884.[95] Furness was first regularly employed by the company in November 1879, according to this letter, and in the five short years since then had designed some 125 buildings and alterations scattered throughout the country, had remodeled the ferryboat *Communipaw*, and had designed and seen built seven sets of passenger and parlor cars. In addition, drawings had been made for other structures that remained unbuilt, and drawings and specifications for a standard passenger car were then on the boards. What a vast amount of work this letter suggests!

From the 1870s on Furness worked not only for the Reading but for the B & O and Pennsylvania railroads as well. The Reading depot for Shamokin, Pennsylvania, of 1876 may be taken as typical of his early work for these clients (fig. 34). The surviving drawing shows a symmetrical design.[96] The high-gabled elevation is articulated by central and end pavilions and a pair of large mullioned and transomed windows. Characteristic of this date, the pavilions are opened by high, pointed arches, and the colorful exterior is broken up into a base of rubble stone beneath smooth stone and diapered brick walls. The B & O depot at Chester of 1886 and the suburban Graver's Lane Reading station of about 1880 show with what invention Furness created a wide variety of picturesque ensembles at the apex of his career. The regularly spaced windows and horizontal hip roof of the Chester station (cat. 27-1) might owe something to Richardson's work, but the explosion of chimneys and clock tower at the skyline shows a rejection by Furness of the taut outline that was the essence of the New England architect's style. A comparison of Chester with Richardson's Union Station at New London, Connecticut, of 1885 dramatized the differences between these contemporary architects. Not to be overlooked at Chester are the elaborate ironwork chimney braces that Furness used repeatedly in his commuter stations. Graver's Lane (cat. 19), with its gawky proportions and histrionic stickwork, is a textbook example of heterogeneous, picturesque composition by accumulation. The core of the station is a rectangle capped by a simple hip roof (cat. 19-3); but the quiet of that form is shattered by the open porte-cochere (cat. 19-1), the shed porch, and above all, the semicircular ticket office tower that breaks outward and upward until it dissolves into a series of gable and shed dormers in a conical roof (cat. 19-5). A bewildering variety of materials, patterns, textures, and colors further enlivens the surface of the building.

This series of commuter and small town stations culminated in the large urban terminals erected just before and after 1890, all of them now gone. Of these the finest was undoubtedly the B & O Station that stood at Twenty-fourth and Chestnut streets in Philadelphia, begun in 1886 (cat. 26); although the largest, most prominent, and most complicated was the Pennsylvania Railroad's Broad Street Station at Market Street, a huge addition to and remodeling (1892–94) of the Wilson Brothers' building of 1881–82 (cat. 33).

Other than to provide symbols within the city for the railway companies, the main concern of the architect of a large terminal was to shape convenient flow patterns for large volumes of pedestrian traffic to and from the trains.

95. In the Historical Society of Pennsylvania.

96. The drawing is dated 1876, so Furness must have done some designing on an irregular basis before the 1879 date of regular salaried employment given in the letter cited above. There is a study for this station in Furness's sketchbook of the mid-1870s.

For a man of Furness's picturesque inclinations it was simple to make the buildings visual nodes within the urban pattern, even one as riotous as that of late nineteenth-century Philadelphia. Dynamic silhouettes, created out of asymmetrical, multi-pronged masses in which one or more towers form visual exclamation points, proclaimed these buildings as entrances into what used to be considered the exciting world of railway travel. In case the traveler missed the architectural point, Karl Bitter was employed at the Broad Street terminal to embody the *Spirit of Transportation* and other appropriate stories in terracotta billboards (cat. 33-6).[97]

Both the B & O and the Broad Street stations were two-level designs, with passengers entering at one level and departing at another. At the Broad Street Station they went up to reach the trains; at the B & O they descended. Chestnut Street at the point where the B & O stood is elevated on concrete and iron preparatory to leaping across the Schuylkill River (cat. 26-2), so one entered the building beneath an elaborately ornamented iron porte-cochère at the second floor (cat. 26-3, left) and descended via broad flights of stairs to track level (cat. 26-9). The entrance was marked by a clock tower, richly outlined and roofed in two stages (cat. 26-1), that may have been suggested by a plate in Viollet-le-Duc (fig. 37). It dominated the acres of roof covering the rest of the station, and anchored the building along the river bank. The skyline was further enriched with dormers, ridge ornaments, and top-heavy chimney stacks. The brick exterior surfaces were pierced by windows of a profuse variety of sizes and shapes: some filled with clear glass, some with colored, some segmental-arched, some round (and those marking the stair towers were stepped and half-arched; cat. 26-5). The result was a case study in Victorian cacophonic massing.

The interior was even more impressive. In the main concourse an exposed iron frame studded with rivet heads articulated the space, while light poured in through huge glass windows upon the ornamental ironwork of the stair railings (cat. 26-9). The fireplaces in the waiting rooms were almost Richardsonian in their employment of massive rock-faced stone voussoirs, but only Furness could have designed the contrast between those voussoirs and the delicate flowers below, or the double fireboxes divided and flanked by brick and stone piers which seemed to compress and buckle beneath the mass of masonry (cat. 26-10, 26-11). Part of that mass was an oversized, solid-brick caricature of a mantel clock. The wanton destruction of this building in the early 1960s knocked a gaping hole in America's Victorian heritage.

Furness has been praised in print several times for the workable plan he provided for the Broad Street Station, but in fact he merely made the arrangement worked out by the Wilson Brothers more responsive to the increased volume of traffic that had developed in the 1880s (cat. 33). Furness's work was a massive enlargement of the existing station, a fairly ordinary Victorian Gothic design on the southwest corner of Broad and Filbert streets, the corner marked by the standard pinnacled clock tower (cat. 33-3, right).[98] The elevated tracks that came in from the west along the south side of Filbert and jumped over Fifteenth Street on a bridge made it necessary to raise the main rooms to the second floor. The ground floor thus became a basement split in two by a covered driveway running east and west for loading and unloading people and baggage from cabs and wagons (fig. 36). Arrival and departure were clearly separated. Departing passengers entered to the north of the driveway, crossed

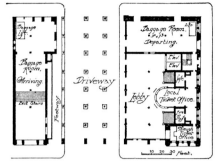

36 Wilson Brothers. Pennsylvania Railroad Station, Philadelphia. 1881–82. Plan (from *AABN*, XVIII, 1885)

97. The *Spirit of Transportation* can now be seen to the left of the ticket counter in Penn-Central's Thirtieth Street Station.

98. Plan, view, and description of the Wilson Brothers' station were published in *AABN*, XVIII, September 26, 1885, p. 150.

the lobby, then mounted stairs flanking the central ticket office to reach the waiting rooms and departure platforms at the upper level. Arriving passengers descended another stairway and entered cabs on the south side of the driveway. Baggage was likewise divided. In short, the Wilson Brothers adequately solved the basic flow patterns required of their station at the time it was designed, but rapidly increased traffic quickly made it too small.

Furness closed the driveway and provided new covered areas for passengers off both Broad and Fifteenth streets (cat. 33-8). He nearly doubled the length of the plan, thus permitting a much larger entrance hall and waiting rooms[99]; but the passenger still arrived under cover, crossed the lobby past the ticket office, then mounted symmetrical, ramped stairs to reach the waiting rooms and trains at the upper level (cat. 33-9). Arrivals exited via stairs now moved south to Market Street (or, when Furness built the Arcade Building across Market Street, via a bridge into that building; cat. 40-2). Arriving and departing baggage were still separated. The enormous office block that rose to the south of the remodeled Wilson Brothers' station spanned Fifteenth Street in continuation of the original arrangement (cat. 33-2). Furness's building was certainly more imposing—with its greater bulk, multipinnacled tower, and sculptural enrichment—than that of the Wilson Brothers, but neither in plan nor in picturesque silhouette did it represent a departure from what they had achieved.

Furness's interiors also outdid in impressiveness the rooms covered with elaborately designed arched trusses in the earlier building. Furness framed his spaces in a rectilinear pattern of ceiling beams and square piers (cat. 33-5). His cubical, additive approach to composition was well exemplified by these piers, in which the raised ornament and elongated consoles on each face failed to turn the corner, but were separated by a reentrant angle. Again we must lament the destruction of a major work of American architecture.

The B & O and the Broad Street stations in Philadelphia form part of a group of large, complex works erected between the mid-eighties and mid-nineties that mark the apex of Furness's career. Others include the Bryn Mawr Hotel, the Williamson School, the later buildings at the Jewish Hospital, and the Library of the University of Pennsylvania. They form as versatile a collection of works as any architect of the period achieved. Furness's creative flame then was burning brightly; it began to subside after the mid-nineties.

The picturesque mass of the Bryn Mawr Hotel of 1890 culminates in a broad cylindrical tower that pierces the sky with an inverted dormer-studded funnel (plate 10). A sizable group of American hotels designed by various architects in the 1880s share this common feature, including such widespread examples as the Bayview Hotel on Jamestown Island off Newport, built about 1885, and the Hotel del Coronado in California of 1886–88. Were they bourgeois reflections of Viollet-le-Duc's restoration of the Château of Pierrefonds? Or did they follow English precedent?

Furness's hotel (now the Baldwin School; cat. 31), built for the Pennsylvania Railroad, replaced a boxy mansarded building designed by the Wilson Brothers. The new building is a long L with rooms off double-loaded corridors (cat. 31-2). From the entrance hall in the rotunda twin stairs sweep around a

99. Published plans of Furness's station do not agree with available interior photographs in all details. The exact arrangement of the station is still in some doubt.

Plate 8 Library, University of Pennsylvania. Tower detail

massive ashlar fireplace (cat. 31-3) to gain the main lobby from which the main stair, supported by iron stringers decorated with rivet heads, rises to the upper floors (cat. 31-5). The exterior of the building is rather like the Williamson School, also going up at this time: textured ashlar fieldstone walls rise to the tops of the fourth-floor window where the deep red brick used in the lower flat arches takes over as the wall material. The basically boxy shape of the building is animated by porches, main and subsidiary towers, chimneys, dormers, and ruddy coloration (cat. 31-1).

The Williamson Free School of Mechanical Trades in Elwyn was finished in 1891 (cat. 30). The complex of buildings at the top of a rise above the railroad is dominated by the main, T-shaped building containing classrooms, administrative offices, dining room, kitchen, and chapel (cat. 30-2). Shops and residences to the left formed the rest of the original layout. The sobriety of the design stems from the relatively limited building budget. As at the Bryn Mawr Hotel, Furness here used a combination of rough-faced fieldstone ashlar and a deep red brick on the exterior of all the buildings. The main building, of a high-waisted design, is belted around the middle by red brick courses at the level of the first-floor arches. The center of the main façade, above the tomb of the donor, is typical of Furness (plate 9). A tall narrow gable in ashlar rises past flanking brick walls set slightly back from the face of the stone. It is pierced by a broad, three-centered arch that is a common form in his work of this period. In the shops he reverted to the austere brick-pier and window architecture of mid-nineteenth century Philadelphia to produce his most restrained design (cat. 30-6).

As we have seen, Furness and Hewitt began the buildings for the Jewish Hospital as early as 1871, and Furness added buildings to the complex in 1888, the late nineties, and after 1900 (cat. 4). The Home for the Aged of 1888 was a variation upon the brick-banded fieldstone work of the contemporary hotel and school. Furness capped its walls with bracketed cornices and mansard roofs, and reverted to the horseshoe arch with exaggerated, striped brick voussoirs (cat. 4-1). As with his red brick buildings of the mid-seventies, Furness's brick-studded fieldstone buildings of the late eighties could be varied according to the desires and the pocketbooks of his clients. The master plan of the hospital that emerged after 1900, like the plan of the Williamson School complex, shows Furness's unsystematic, even haphazard, approach to site planning (cat. 4-2).

These large-scale designs of about 1890 culminated in the library building Furness executed for the University of Pennsylvania (cat. 29). It was commissioned by a building committee chaired by his brother Horace; the cornerstone was laid in October 1888; and the structure opened for use in February 1891. Although significantly altered, the library survives as the Furness Building on Thirty-fourth Street in the heart of the campus. It is not only one of the masterworks of American Victorian design, but occupies an important niche in the evolution of library architecture in this country as well.

Like Memorial Hall at Harvard and other significant Victorian buildings, the vaguely ecclesiastical exterior of the building belies a workable plan (cat. 29-5). The parts of the program were separated analytically according to the method of the École des Beaux-Arts, and each is given its own external expression. The core of the plan was the reading room, originally four stories high (cat. 29-18), reached from an entrance hall containing a monumental iron stairway (cat.

29-10). The hall itself was entered from a freestanding, open porch (cat. 29-1). The main reading space was surrounded on the remaining three sides by a lower reading area with apsidal study alcoves (cat. 29-17), the cataloguing department and offices, and, to the south, the delivery room and stacks.

The building was praised at the time of its design for its utilitarian arrangement —something that is difficult to understand today, given the present condition of the building and subsequent experience in library design. All of the books were gathered out of sight in the stack area. Although we now take this arrangement for granted, the library in which readers were kept to one area and books housed in a separate unit was very new in the 1880s—so new that Horace Furness, in his address at the opening of the library, could only wonder at the innovation:

> the best . . . is where the books . . . are stored, or, to use a name coined by Mr. Winsor, and now generally adopted, the "book-stack." Here . . . the problem has been triumphantly solved of the greatest possible light, of an equable temperature, and of absolute indestructibility. Its indestructibility is assured in that it is built entirely of bricks, iron and glass. Nothing but a cataclysm that will turn Earth's base to stubble can harm it or its contents. Its glass roof catches every ray of Heaven's light, and pours it into every nook and corner. . . . There is room in it . . . for about 300,000 books, and when this number is stored there . . . the rear wall can be taken down and the stack indefinitely prolonged. . . . Thus there is provision for the present and prevision for the future, and our whole building may stand as a model of the happy employment of means to ends.[100]

From the Middle Ages to the nineteenth century, libraries had relatively small collections and few users. They usually took the form of overgrown gentlemen's studies: comfortable, book-lined rooms in which the books were all visible and within arm's reach of the reader. Furness's own Library Company building of the previous decade had carried on that tradition. With the emergence of the large national, public, and university libraries in the nineteenth century this system became totally inadequate; at the British Museum and the Bibliothèques Ste. Geneviève and Nationale, in the middle of the century, central storage in a stack area was introduced. The books were collected on self-supporting metal shelving, usually structurally independent of the building itself, and were brought out to the reader for use at the library or for home borrowing.

The stack was not introduced to the United States until 1877, when it was used in Ware and Van Brunt's addition to Gore Hall in Cambridge at the urging of Harvard's librarian[101]—the same Justin Winsor whom Horace Furness mentioned in his address. Thereafter the stack system became an accepted way of handling book storage in large libraries. The Furnesses undoubtedly consulted Winsor, Ware, and the new Harvard library before designing the library at Pennsylvania, although Furness did not repeat the brittle Gothic exterior of the Gore Hall addition.

The shed roofs of Furness's stack were of glass (cat. 29-7, right), as are the walkways between shelves at each level. As Horace remarked, this would flood the stack area with natural light. Over the years these glass roofs have been covered, and it would be hard to convince the graduate students who now use this dingy space that it was ever bright and cheerful. Horace mentioned the potential flexibility of the stack; this caught the eye of others as well. Writing in the *Library Journal* before ground had even been broken for the new

100. *Proceedings at the Opening of the Library of the University of Pennsylvania,* February 7, 1891, Philadelphia, 1891.

101. William Jordy, "The Beaux-Arts Renaissance: Charles McKim's Boston Public Library," in his *American Buildings and Their Architects,* vol. III, *Progressive and Academic Ideals at the Turn of the Twentieth Century,* New York, 1972, pp. 314 ff. The Gore Hall stacks were published in *AABN,* III, November 23, 1878.

building, Talcott Williams praised it for its workability and flexibility. The stack, he wrote, "admits of indefinite expansion to the south by extending the stack a bay at a time, the end wall being moved out on jack-screws"[102] (cat. 29-6). This never happened. The erection of the Duhring Wing to the south of the library in 1914 eliminated any possibility of the expansion envisioned by Furness.

In the design of the library Furness brought together English, French, and American sources to create an uncompromising masterpiece. When it was built (and for many years afterward), the library despite its round-arched openings was called Gothic, or Victorian Gothic, in style. Its picturesque and cacophonic massing of individual features (including a Palladian window!); its combination of materials of varied colors and textures; and its terra-cotta ornament, ranging from minutely observed natural foliage to abstract, almost surreal, terminals that again stand comparison with the work of Antonio Gaudí: all of these are familiar aspects of English Victorian design. In addition, Ruskin would have approved of the exterior of the south wall of the stacks, now covered by the Duhring Wing, because its design recalled the façade of an Italian Romanesque church (cat. 29-2). Finally, the overscaled window in the main tower (plate 8), which floods the stairway with western light, seems directly related to Mould's parsonage at All Souls' in New York, an Anglophile work Furness remembered from his student days (fig. 13).

Although a round-arched Gothic was possible in the nineteenth century, Furness's use of such arches suggests a second source of inspiration. A glance at the broad, repeating stone arches on the lower exterior walls of the stack wing (cat. 29-3), or of the low-sprung arches on stubby columns that divide the reading area (cat. 29-17), indicates that Furness had been looking at Richardson's work, perhaps in the pages of the Van Rensselaer monograph which appeared while the library was being designed. The ecclesiastical plan of the library follows that of Richardson's Billings Library at the University of Vermont, sketches of which appear in the monograph, although Furness's library was for that time functionally far in advance of Richardson's, which had no stack area.

Even more important, especially in the interior of the library, was the influence of Viollet-le-Duc. The form and details of the freestanding iron stairway in the tower (cat. 29-14) must have been inspired by a design for a Hôtel de Ville in the *Entretiens* (fig. 37), while the decorative details of the massive fireplace in the main reading room are dependent upon similar details in another view of the same design (fig. 35). But even more in the spirit of Viollet, and completely characteristic of Furness in execution, is the overhead structure of the apsidal reading room with its exposed, radiating, curved iron beams decorated with rivet heads. Furness's sense of humor appears in the detail where these beams meet the wall (cat. 29-17). The horizontal members curve down toward brick pilasters . . . but never meet them. Instead, the pilasters are sloped back to the wall, and the massive iron beams bring their full load down upon delicate terra-cotta leaves! Rather than load being visually received by support, which would produce a feeling of stability in the viewer, Furness's detail destroys all sense of equilibrium. We are forced to partake in the conflict of forces

37 E.-E. Viollet-le-Duc. "Hôtel de Ville" (from *Entretiens: Atlas*, 1864, Pl. XXIII)

Plate 9 Williamson Free School of Mechanical Trades.
Main building from south

102. Talcott Williams, "Plans for the Library of the University of Pennsylvania," *Library Journal*, August 13, 1888, pp. 237–243.

38 McKim, Mead and White. Public Library, Boston. 1888-92. Photograph by Jean Baer O'Gorman

unresolved here, as we were in his earlier banks, and the result is as dynamically unsettling.

At the apex of his career Furness drew upon all of his resources to create for the University of Pennsylvania one of his finest works. Unfortunately for his reputation, this occurred at a time when American architecture was beginning a transformation which would take it far from the picturesque ideal of the post-Civil War years. Furness's library was begun in 1888, the same year in which McKim, Mead and White began the Boston Public Library (fig. 38). In his article on the University Library, Talcott Williams may have praised the workability of Furness's design and condemned the expense and unworkability of McKim's, but stylistically McKim's work was to dominate the immediate future. Merging Richardson's example at the Marshall Field Wholesale Store with a renewed interest in Renaissance classicism, as William Jordy has shown, McKim prepared the way for the disciplined architectural style that was to bury Furness's work in obscurity for the next fifty years.

## 9. Last Years (c. 1895-1912)

With few exceptions, the works that issued from the office of Furness, Evans and Company from the late nineties on seem now of less interest than the works of the seventies and eighties—for several reasons other than the current state of our taste. First, Furness's work of the seventies and eighties was relatively small scale and personal. In the nineties his office grew in size, and the scale and volume of work increased to a point where no one man could control every detail. More and more, as time progressed, the buildings of Furness, Evans and Company were turned out by the "company." Then, too, by the nineties the general architectural situation had changed, and we must view Furness's later work against a backdrop quite different from that of the seventies or eighties. More significant work was being done by Louis Sullivan and the Chicago School, by Frank Lloyd Wright and the Prairie School, or by Charles F. McKim and Stanford White and their followers.[103] Furness's attempts to work within the new framework seem unsuccessful. Finally, there are personal factors to be considered. Furness reached the zenith of his creative powers at the B & O and Broad Street stations and the University Library. Thereafter, he appears to have been less sure of himself. And increasingly he turned his attention from the design in hand to reminiscing about his wartime heroics.

Furness's toying with Richardsonian motifs around 1890 signals the beginning of his decline. For his own country house in Media (fig. 39) he shrank the plan of the contemporary University Library, and erected over it a stone, brick, and shingle house with eyebrow dormers that owed much to Richardson's domestic work. A second commission by the university resulted in an unexecuted design for an Alumni Memorial Hall.[104] The auditorium was to be polygonal in plan, and have exterior walls of brick and terra-cotta above a rock-faced stone base. This was to be fronted by a triangular pediment rising above a Richardsonian porte-cochere opened with heavy, low-sprung arches. The Chapel at Mount Sinai Cemetery, designed in 1891, has a high, hipped, red tile roof surmounting walls of horizontally banded grey stone and red terra-cotta (cat. 32-1). The shape of the roof is close to that of Richardson's parish house at Trinity Church, Boston. The curious windows, cut back at the top to form circles, are not simply repetitions of the Islamic arches used by Furness in other work for the Jewish community; they are in fact very similar to the windows in the upper story of the main front of Richardson's Ames Memorial Town Hall at North

103. See note 101.
104. *PI*, October 27, 1890, p. 6; *PRERBG*, VI, no. 1, January 1891. Illustrated in the *Architectural Era*, February 1891, and Massey 3, Pl. 4.

Easton, Massachusetts.[105] Furness undoubtedly had studied Richardson's work in Mrs. Van Rensselaer's monograph of 1888, or in the portfolios dedicated to Richardson that were published in Boston in the mid-1880s.[106]

In the University Library Furness had controlled his use of Richardsonian motifs, altering and mingling them with other, more familiar sources. In the Alumni Hall the design breaks into its component parts before our eyes. Furness's sense of design was so distinctly his own that his playing with Richardsonian forms suggests a loss of direction. His brief flirtation with so alien a source was the first indication of his declining powers.

Among the most important works of these last years were the large commercial buildings erected by the firm in center city, including the Franklin Building of 1894–95, the West End Trust Building of 1898, 1901, and the Arcade (Commercial Trust) Building of 1900, 1904, and 1913. All have been destroyed. The seven-story Franklin Building on South Twelfth Street was a layered terra-cotta wedding cake decorated with caryatids attributed to Karl Bitter and a continuous balcony at the level of the fourth floor (cat. 35). It lacked that sense of purpose which marks Sullivan's contemporary Guaranty Building in Buffalo. Such a comparison is not without meaning, because Furness seems to have had an eye on the work of his former assistant. The West End Trust, built of red granite, Pompeian brick, and terra-cotta, was one of Furness's last exercises in polychromy (cat. 39). It rose fourteen stories from a small lot on South Penn Square. Above a two-story, ground-floor arcade continuous oriels stretched up to gabled dormers in a mansard roof. It looked like an elaboration of a section of Sullivan's Chicago Stock Exchange of 1893–94, but such a comparison merely points up the wide gulf that had opened between master and former draftsman. The thirteen-story Arcade Building (cat. 40), which was joined to the Broad Street Station by a bridge across Market Street, was given an exterior rectangular articulation of recessed piers and molded spandrels that adequately expressed the skeletal frame within (cat. 40-2). But comparison with Sullivan's coeval Carson, Pirie & Scott Store is inevitable, and again Sullivan's building seems the more accomplished. The apparent massiveness of the Arcade belied the fact that it was a mere screen, one bay deep, above the Fifteenth Street side walk (cat. 40-1). This screen, the bridge across Market Street, and the building's proximity to Broad Street Station, City Hall, and the West End Trust gave Furness's work at the Arcade an urbanistic role of far greater importance than can be adequately appreciated now that only City Hall remains (cat. 40-7).

Among the more satisfactory smaller works of the period were the Jayne House of 1895, the Merion Cricket Club of 1892–96, and the Philadelphia Saving Fund Society Building on Washington Square, an addition to and remodeling of 1897–98 of Addison Hutton's earlier building. The Jayne House is one of the most imposing surviving town houses of Victorian Philadelphia (cat. 37). The exterior, of textured red terra-cotta and red brick, drips with heavy floral ornament, while the dormer gables contain terra-cotta *putti* cast from molds used at Broad Street Station (cat. 37-6). The interior is no more domestic in scale than the exterior. The entrance gives access either to the former doctor's office to the left, or up a broad flight of steps to an expansive two-story, top-lighted well of space surrounded by a gallery at the upper level and focused upon a stair that winds around the fireplace (cat. 37-2). The flues are split to either side of a tall arched opening, from which a curved balustrade projects

39 Furness, Evans and Co. Furness House ("Idlewild"), Media, Pennsylvania. c. 1888. Photograph by Cervin Robinson

105. Clearly shown in the portfolio *Ames Memorial Building[s] North Easton, Mass.*, Monographs of American Architecture, III, Boston, 1886.

106. See also note 67.

40 Allen Evans and McKim, Mead and White (with Frank Furness). Girard Trust Company, Philadelphia. 1905–7. (Furness, Evans and Co.'s West End Trust, of 1898 and 1901, with skyline altered, is to the right; their Morris Building, 1909–10, to the left.) Photograph by Frank Taylor. Courtesy Historical Society of Pennsylvania, Philadelphia

out over the fireplace. The original effect of this interior has been somewhat altered by the loss of the mantel shelf and the former dark, patterned wallpaper, but it still commands attention. Here Furness returned to the skylighted open space he had used with such success in earlier work (cat. 37-1). The result is equally fine, but in other instances where he reused former motifs the results proved less satisfactory.

The ruddiness of the Merion Cricket Club contrasts sharply with the deep green of its well-trimmed tennis lawns (cat. 34-2). A rambling building capped by a multigabled red tile roof, the main feature of the exterior is the arcaded porch. The exterior materials are textured red terra-cotta and red brick, as on the Jayne House. Above the semicircular and three-centered arches of the porch and porte-cochere are terra-cotta plaques depicting cricket bats, golf clubs, and tennis rackets (cat. 34-4). The building is a spacious and comfortable—if unexceptional—home for the club, whose leadership included Allen Evans.

The remodeling of the Philadelphia Saving Fund Society Building is more remarkable (cat. 38). The extension of the façade on Walnut Street followed the style of Addison Hutton's original building (cat. 38-5, 38-6). Within, Piranesian arches span the banking room, which despite later alterations remains one of the finest spaces in Furness's oeuvre (cat. 38-2).[107] But the year was 1897, and such an achievement had become rare. Furness was only fifty-eight, but he was past his prime as a major force in Philadelphia architectural design.

Furness had received instruction in classical design from Hunt, although with the exception of an occasional personalized Palladian window, he never designed anything specifically classical during the height of his powers. In the late nineties it appears that he turned to this unfamiliar style in an effort to keep up with his East Coast contemporaries. He was not very successful. William R. Ware wrote to him early in 1898 thanking him for copies of his project for the Pennsylvania State Capitol, but his remarks on the designs were not encouraging: "They show how much can be done, even in unfamiliar fields, by a practiced hand. But they also show, as I wrote to Horace, how impossible it is really to hit the spirit of one style when all one's experience is in another."[108]

The letter is full of such ambivalent valuations of Furness's work: not even his old atelier mate could accept his buildings without reservation. "I see their merit, but they are too unusual to be agreeable. . . . I feel about them very much as I do about Sullivan's work. . . . All the same your work & his seem to me the best examples of work done out of hand or, rather, out of one's head, without regard to use & custom."[109] We may find the comparison with Sullivan complimentary from our point of view, but it is doubtful that Ware meant it entirely that way. His letter could not have cheered a failing Furness.

Nor could the history of the commission for the Girard Trust Bank on South Broad Street (fig. 40), a building eventually erected (1905–7) on the model of the Roman Pantheon. Official credit for the design went to Allen Evans and McKim, Mead and White. Although Furness played a significant role in the planning of this building, he did so without the client's knowledge.[110] He must have been stung when E. B. Morris, president of Girard Bank, wrote to Allen

107. The treads of the stairway to the balcony in P.S.F.S. are covered with interlocking tiles designed by Furness. His sketchbooks are filled with these patterns.

108. This letter, like the documentation for all that follows, is in the possession of George Wood Furness.

109. Ware goes on to request copies of Furness's work, but it is unlikely that he received them. Adolf K. Placzek, Avery Librarian at Columbia, can find no trace there of any Furness material. I thank him for looking.

110. A sketch plan of the bank and a sworn statement by Furness (both in the possession of George Wood Furness) prove that he did indeed have a hand in this design. The plan is dated 1903–4, but that would seem to be too early.

Plate 10 Bryn Mawr Hotel. Entrance tower from west

Evans on June 16, 1904, asking him to submit a proposal for the building, because Furness was specifically excluded: "My interest is in you and not your firm; for while I have the highest respect and esteem for Mr. Furness, we do not wish a building designed upon his well-known lines. I say this without the slightest reference to Mr. Furness's great ability and skill as an architect. . . ." The objection was to Furness as a designer. Since Furness's career had been built upon his ability to please bankers and other businessmen, we could find no more reliable witness to his fading star.

In these last years Furness and his friends began to dwell upon his Civil War record, almost to the exclusion of his architectural achievements. He now liked to be called "Captain" Furness, and his most extensive obituary was published by the Military Order of the Loyal Legion of the United States (1913). At the height of his powers Furness had shown little interest in receiving recognition for his military exploits, but in August 1899, perhaps in a moment of nostalgia for military life caused by the Spanish-American War, he was petitioning Congress for its highest military award, and trying to find old comrades who would substantiate his claim (see p. 19). In 1905 he spent much time trying to locate a former Confederate soldier he had once helped on the battlefield. Instead of an active architect, he had become an "old soldier."

Frank Furness lived until 1912; several of his last years were spent in ill health. They must not have been happy ones, and his reputation as a disagreeable person was accordingly enhanced. He died in near obscurity, amid his flowers and horses at "Idlewild." The local papers barely mentioned that he had been an architect—and thus began a neglect that was to last for half a century.

## 10. Furness and His Critics (1876–1973)

When H. H. Richardson died in April 1886 he was at the peak of a very influential career, and the international architectural press was flooded with the news of his demise. Within two years Mrs. Van Rensselaer's handsome monograph on the man and his work was published by Houghton Mifflin. Richardson has remained in the limelight ever since.

When Frank Furness died in Media, Pennsylvania, on June 27, 1912, he was long past his prime, and his passing went almost unnoticed in the architectural press. The local papers that carried his obituary mentioned a few of his buildings, but were content to devote more space to his illustrious father and brother, and his recognized bravery during the Civil War.[111]

Whatever recognition and praise Furness's work attracted in the first half of the twentieth century came mainly from Philadelphia architects and critics. Until recently outsiders have largely ignored or condemned it. A few laudatory notices in the seventies and eighties in the national press were followed even before his death by pejorative criticism. The recent rise in Furness's stock is a function of the "changing ideals in modern architecture," to use the title of Peter Collins's book,[112] and any attempt to understand the vicissitudes of his reputation must take into account these changes. It must also take into account the fact that Philadelphia architects have played a significant role in recent shifts in architectural theory and taste.

Philadelphia architecture was of national interest at the time of the Centennial Exhibition of 1876. We have already seen that the anonymous critic of the *American Architect* in that year saw in Furness a "clever, original, and brilliant

111. Obituaries appeared in the *Philadelphia Bulletin*, the *Inquirer*, and the *Public Ledger*. The only professional notice we have found is the *Philadelphia Real Estate Record and Builders' Guide* for July 3, 1912, which quotes the *Ledger* account and mentions Furness's most important works.

112. London, 1965. Collins does not share the recent appreciation of Furness's work (cf. pp. 246–247).

architect" whose work was "full of life," "the work of an architect full of spirit and invention"; this, despite the fact that the same critic lamented Furness's want of control. His work "only needs the chastening of its exuberances into sobriety and repose, to earn for its author a higher rank."[113] This set the pattern of Furness criticism, for it was just this exuberance that made earlier twentieth-century critics grimace, and makes present students ecstatic.

After around 1880 almost all recognition of his existence disappeared from the Boston-based *American Architect.* But he was too important an architect to be entirely ignored during his lifetime, and other periodicals such as the *Brick-builder* or Philadelphia-based *Architectural Era,* among professional journals, and the *Scientific American,* among general magazines, did carry his work from time to time. Criticism began to run against him in the nineties. In 1888 Talcott Williams in the *Library Journal,* a publication dedicated to fighting expensive and unworkable library design, had found the University Library to be very workable, and economically more justified than Boston's coeval and very expensive Public Library.[114] By 1897, however, A. R. Willard, in an article on college libraries in the *New England Magazine,* was merely condescending, noting that "at the time [it was erected it was] the finest structure of its kind in the country," but that "such a design would not now be approved by architects and connoisseurs. . . ."[115] So quickly had one of Furness's major works become obsolete.

His work was as obsolete stylistically as it was functionally. Four years before his death it was torn to shreds by Huger Elliot in the *Architectural Record.*[116] In an article on Philadelphia that is generally disapproving, Elliot singled out Furness's work (without naming the architect) for some of his most stinging barbs. One after another the major works fell: "Broad Street Station, of an unrelieved and unpleasant red, lifts pseudo-Gothic towers and pinnacles to the sky; the detail, particularly in the interior, is of a kind to make the judicious weep." The façade of the Pennsylvania Academy, "in the Victorian Gothic, or something else, is weird and strange. It is only surpassed by the Library of the University of Pennsylvania, the 'fortified greenhouse,' than which nothing more grotesque could be imagined." And Elliot summed up Furness's national reputation at the beginning of the twentieth century: "these buildings and others of less importance in the debasement of public taste are relics of the low-water mark in American architecture." Elliot's appraisal of Furness's work was echoed in 1917 in a survey of Philadelphia architecture written by William F. Gray.[117] Gray had faint praise for Rodef Shalom's "bulbous dome," but he assigned its design to George Hewitt. The Gothic Revival had moved into a new, more archaeological phase following the latitudinarianism of the post–Civil War years, and Gray lamented the fact that the University Library was erected before the days of the more accurate Cope and Stewardson or Frank Miles Day:

It is unfortunate that the change in regime did not take place a few years earlier, as we would have been spared the so-called Library Building with its raw, ugly color, its "original" design and awkward plan and wild and obtrusive "ornament."

Nor did Furness's other public buildings please him more.

The Academy of Fine Arts is an essay in an original style which returns to first principles, but in its defiance of certain fundamental principles of abstract design and of construction has almost entirely failed. The combination of pointed and segmental arches. The division of the portal by a

113. See note 62.

114. See note 102.

115. A. R. Willard, "College Libraries in the United States," *New England Magazine,* n.s. XVII, September 1897–February 1898, pp. 438–439.

116. Huger Elliot, "Architecture in Philadelphia," *Architectural Record,* XXIII, April 1908, pp. 294 ff.

117. W. F. Gray, "Philadelphia's Architecture," *Philadelphia History,* Philadelphia, 1917, pp. 317 ff.

pillar, which conveys the impression of a prop for a ruptured arch, and the use as a central motive, of a mutilated classic figure, the character of which is known only to a few, are things which would defeat any design. Any architectural feature which is not self-explanatory is wrong.

Furness's extension to the Broad Street Station "dreadfully mutilated" the Wilson Brothers' original design. Finally, the Provident is characterized as "an ogre's castle in a fairy story."

As early as 1870 Furness's father had warned the A.I.A. that the architect would be in trouble with his critics if he designed buildings that were not easily understandable, and Gray confirms this in his remarks about the Academy. Furness's use of apparently inexplicable detail had jarred the critic's complacency.

In the 1920s two people who had known him well spoke admiringly of Furness and his work. Louis Sullivan's praise for his first real mentor was published in 1924. His remarks were noticed in the *Philadelphia Evening Bulletin* in April, and immediately augmented in the same paper the next day by Albert Kelsey.[118] For Kelsey, a Philadelphia architect, Furness was "an original genius of dominating personality" who endured "more scathing criticism" than his fellow architects: "in his lifetime it became a sort of fad among critics to scoff at his works." But at the height of his powers Furness was equal to it.

> Never for a moment would he brook interference with his plans and neither client nor critic would be spared if he saw fit to speak his mind plainly on any subject. He could swear like a trooper. With pungent wit and a caustic tongue he challenged and invited criticism.

If his work was eccentric, this was a function of his "masterful domineering, fearless and aggressive" personality. "Furness was too good an architect not to know what he was doing and I sometimes think that some of the oddities he introduced were merely the rebellion of a freedom-loving soul that refused to be bound by rules." Oddities, we remember, were what his father had called for at the beginning of his career.

Yet even Kelsey could not accept the Library at the University of Pennsylvania, which, he felt, was "absolutely ridiculous and without rhyme or reason." To these friendly if ambivalent voices were added a few others such as Lewis Mumford, who in the *Brown Decades* (1931) was sympathetic enough to call Furness's work "bold, unabashed, ugly, and yet somehow healthily pregnant."

But these were isolated accolades. When Furness was mentioned by other than Philadelphians, which was rare, it was either because of Sullivan's kind words, as in Henry-Russell Hitchcock's *Modern Architecture* (1929), or in order to condemn his age. Talbot Hamlin, for example, in *The American Spirit in Architecture* (1926) used the Provident to flog the entire era:

> Like so much American Victorian Gothic the sense of scale is absolutely lacking: what should be small is big, and vice versa. Structural logic—the foundation of Gothic—is forgotten. Stumpy polished granite columns; arches, cusped, pointed and segmental; offsets, brackets and meaning- less gigantic moldings are piled together in astonishing ways. Such build- ings are obvious proofs that the original is not always beautiful. It is tragic that the conscious desire to create beauty, which was vividly alive through- out this era produced so little that was lovely; and created for so many an

118. Albert Kelsey, "Men and Things," *Philadelphia Evening Bulletin*, April 18, 1924, p. 8, col. 5.

70

environment of such meretricious ugliness.

It would take another generation to find these same characteristics positive rather than pejorative features of Victorian building.

What is noticeable about all of these early critics is their ability to zero in upon the essential features of Furness's work and condemn them for being what they were. But what these critics found to be bad Gothic can now be viewed as some of the most successful and challenging of Victorian building. This dramatic change came about after the Second World War. Furness's work remained the same, but two new factors had emerged to produce a more tolerant attitude toward it: a revisionistic critical stance and, more significantly, an approving architectural theory. We are concerned with the second here.

Architects and critics of all persuasions in the first half of the twentieth century could look back at Richardson's work without wincing. They could see the work of their day descending from his, either by way of Sullivan and Wright, or of Charles McKim. Much of early twentieth-century architecture was a classicizing style that owed something to Richardson's disciplining of the picturesque in the 1880s. In 1936 the Museum of Modern Art published Henry-Russell Hitchcock's monograph on *The Architecture of H. H. Richardson and His Times.* Furness was almost totally forgotten.[119]

Thirty years later, however, Mies van der Rohe's slogan "Less is More," the succinct statement of classical control, had been answered by Robert Venturi's "Less is a Bore," the succinct rebuttal of one whose taste is for the eclectic and the picturesque. In his much-discussed *Complexity and Contradiction in Architecture* (1966) Venturi attacked the International Style—the classicizing architecture of the 1920s through the 1950s—because it was incapable of expressing "the richness and ambiguity of modern experience," and from that Ruskinian platform stated his preference for architecture that showed "messy vitality" rather than "obvious unity." In short, Venturi defended the kind of compositional complexity that was characteristic of much Victorian architecture. Nor was he alone. *Complexity and Contradiction* was but one verbal formulation of a broad movement, known internationally as the New Brutalism, that began after the Second World War. Louis Kahn's Richards Medical Research Facility at the University of Pennsylvania (1959), a bristling cluster of vertical stacks, and Venturi's own work stand as declarations of faith in the picturesque. Both Kahn and Venturi are Philadelphians working in Furness's city, and not incidentally, Furness was rediscovered as the historical precedent for the "Philadelphia School" branch of Brutalist building.[120]

Venturi's book contains several sympathetic remarks about Furness's Pennsylvania Academy and National Bank of the Republic. The latter, for example,

> contained an array of violent pressures within a rigid frame. The half-segmental arch, blocked by the submerged tower which, in turn, bisects the façade into a near duality, and the violent adjacencies of rectangles, squares, lunettes, and diagonals of contrasting sizes, compose a building seemingly held up by the buildings next door: it is an almost insane short story of a castle on a city street.

This quotation not only shows that the present essay owes much to Venturi's vision, but that his vision, when compared to Talbot Hamlin's exemplified above, represents only one major change. The context of Venturi's statement shows that he *likes* the very conflicts that Hamlin condemned. And Venturi's own work

119. Furness is mentioned once in Hitchcock's work on Richardson. His "bold vagaries" are said to have inspired Sullivan's (corrupt) early work. (In the 1961 edition Hitchcock noted that "inspired" should be merely "encouraged," and suggested that even that might be too definite.)

120. In 1969 the Philadelphia Chapter, American Institute of Architects, bestowed on Furness its Centennial Award of Honor as the "Philadelphia Architect of the Past." Louis Kahn received the award for living architects.

41 Robert Venturi (Venturi and Rauch in association with Cope and Lippincott). Guild House, Philadelphia. 1960–63. Photograph by Cervin Robinson

of the sixties was indebted to the example of Furness, as a comparison of his Guild House in Philadelphia of 1960–63 (fig. 41) with the main building at Williamson School (cat. 30-2) will serve to indicate.

Venturi's critical appreciation of Furness was floated on a wave of sympathetic historical writing that had begun at the local level. As early as 1943 John Harbeson, a prominent Philadelphia architect, wrote in the *Pennsylvania Magazine of History* that Furness was "the one who was responsible for the best architecture of the period," although he immediately followed that encomium with the qualification that "it is true that he did some of the worst also."[121]

However, it is more significant, if incorrect, that Harbeson saw Furness as a forerunner of the architecture of his own day:

> Furness's work was original, independent in conception, and in it may be found the germs of much contemporary architectural thought. [Furness] may . . . be considered as the architectural godfather of Louis Sullivan, the spiritual grandfather of Frank Lloyd Wright and of the so-called International movement in architecture.

Only parochialism can account for the myopia that caused this Philadelphia admirer to see a nonexistent connection between Furness's work and the International Style.

Eight years later, in 1951, William Campbell, another Philadelphia architect who really fathered the Furness revival among historians as Venturi was to do among critics, put together the first attempt to understand Furness historically,[122] and this was followed by a series of local publications. In 1953, *Philadelphia Architecture in the Nineteenth Century,* edited by yet another Philadelphia architect, Theo White, treated no less than seven of Furness's buildings sympathetically; and Professor Robert C. Smith of the University of Pennsylvania, in an article published by the American Philosophical Society,[123] called Furness "Philadelphia's greatest architect of the late nineteenth century and one of the pioneers of the modern movement in America." By the 1960s younger Philadelphia architects and scholars, most notably James C. Massey, had begun the long, tedious task of reconstructing and publishing Furness's forgotten oeuvre.[124]

Campbell's article was published in the English *Architectural Review* and first brought international attention to Furness's work. He presented Furness as a major Victorian architect unjustly forgotten by the architectural world, and repeated Harbeson's linking of Furness to Sullivan and Wright. Thereafter Furness could no longer be historically isolated. Like Richardson, Sullivan, and Wright, he now belonged to the club. In the *New Yorker* in 1957 Lewis Mumford updated his stamp of approval, journalistically touting Furness's Provident building as "nothing less than a second Declaration of Independence." Furness had "pushed ugliness to the point where it almost turned into beauty, or at least a brutal creativity,"[125] thus in the national press linking Furness to the "Brutalists" even before the work of Kahn and Venturi had reached a national audience. In 1958 Henry-Russell Hitchcock included the Provident in his monumental and basic *Architecture: Nineteenth and Twentieth Centuries,* and by 1960 Furness had become the subject of a feature article in the popular professional journal, the *Architectural Forum.*[126] The sixties saw Furness's reputation reach such heights that theses were being written about him at eastern universities.[127]

121. John Harbeson, "Philadelphia's Victorian Architecture," *Pennsylvania Magazine of History,* XXLVII, July 1943, pp. 266 ff.

122. See note 89.

123. R. C. Smith, "Two Centuries of Philadelphia Architecture," *Historic Philadelphia,* Philadelphia, 1953, p. 303.

124. See note 82 and the list of abbreviated references. Massey's full-scale monograph on Furness is awaited.

125. Reprinted in Lewis Mumford, *The Highway and the City,* New York, 1963, p. 203.

126. "Fearless Frank Furness," *Architectural Forum,* June 1960, pp. 109 ff.

127. Such as an undergraduate thesis at Princeton by Charles Savage and a master's thesis at Yale by Neil Levine.

With the exception of Mumford, these historical revisionists had misrepresented the nature of Furness's influence. Campbell ended his *Architectural Review* article by echoing Harbeson: "to reach Wright, Sullivan was necessary, and to reach Sullivan perhaps Furness," a cautious linkage of Furness with the American masters of the late nineteenth century. In 1957 R. P. Adams threw caution to the wind, declaring, out of a lack of understanding rather than truth, that Sullivan had learned more from Furness than from Richardson.[128] Sullivan had certainly founded his ornamental style upon that of Furness, but he derived his fundamental attitude toward architectural form from an intense examination of Richardson's work. Of the two, Richardson's example was the more immediately important, for through Sullivan it profoundly and directly affected the early work of Frank Lloyd Wright.[129] The impact of Furness's work was to lie fallow for half a century.

Although Richardson was without argument the more immediately influential of the two, this exhibition, mounted by a Philadelphia institution some sixty years after Furness's death and seven years after Venturi's manifesto, makes it clear that Furness can no longer be denied his rightful place as one of America's most significant builders. His reputation has been rescued and his place in the history of American architecture assured. It is sad that so many of his finest works have not survived to bear witness to his new historical stature.

128. R. P. Adams, "Architecture and the Romantic Tradition," *American Quarterly*, IX, 1957, pp. 46 ff.

129. J. F. O'Gorman, "Henry Hobson Richardson and Frank Lloyd Wright," *Art Quarterly*, XXXII, Autumn 1969, pp. 292 ff.

Demolition of the Provident Life and Trust Company, 1959. Photograph by Penelope Hartshorne

# Catalogue of Selected Buildings

George E. Thomas and James F. O'Gorman

## 1 Church of the Holy Apostles (now Shiloh Baptist Church)

**Twenty-first and Christian Streets**
**Fraser, Furness and Hewitt**

Commissioned in February 1868 and opened in December 1870, the church was largely the work of George Hewitt, who later altered the entrance (1890) and erected the tower (1891). The commission included a Sunday school, finished in 1873. The chancel has been remodeled, and the roof structure propped by longitudinal steel trusses.

References: *Pl*, July 10, 1890, p. 7; William Casner, *History of the Church of the Holy Apostles, 1868–1918*, Philadelphia, n.d., pp. 19, 75.
See plate 1

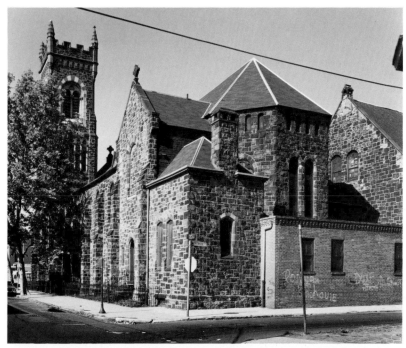

1–2 Exterior of the apse from southwest

1–3 Nave, roof trusses

1–1 (opposite) Exterior from north

2-1 Interior facing tabernacle. Courtesy Congregation Rodeph
Shalom, Philadelphia

## 2 Rodef Shalom Synagogue

**Broad and Mt. Vernon Streets**
**Fraser, Furness and Hewitt**

Cornerstone laid July 1869. The building was consecrated in September 1870, and finished by June 1871. Demolished 1927.

References: *Specifications. Synagogue for the Congregation Rodef Sholam [sic]*, Philadelphia, 1869; *Proceedings of the Laying of the Corner-Stone for the Synagogue . . . Rodef Shalom*, Philadelphia, 1869; *AABN*, I, January 29, 1876, p. 40; Rachel Wischnitzer, *Synagogue Architecture in the United States*, Philadelphia, 1955, pp. 76–77; Tatum, pp. 101, 190.

2-2 Exterior from northwest. Color lithograph by Benjamin Linfoot, 1869. Historical Society of Pennsylvania, Philadelphia

2-4 Chairs. Collection Congregation Rodeph Shalom, Philadelphia

2-3 Tabernacle. Courtesy Congregation Rodeph Shalom, Philadelphia

3-1 Exterior from northeast. *c.* 1880. Courtesy Pennsylvania
Academy of the Fine Arts, Philadelphia

## 3 Pennsylvania Academy of the Fine Arts

**Broad and Cherry Streets**
**Furness and Hewitt**

An "Invitation for Proposals," dated June 20, 1871, and calling for designs by November 1, was sent to a number of Philadelphia architects. Drawings were received from Furness and Hewitt (the invitation had been sent to Fraser, Furness and Hewitt, but Fraser left the firm in September), Henry A. Sims, Addison Hutton, and Thomas W. Richards. The cornerstone of Furness and Hewitt's building was laid in December 1872, and the dedication took place in April 1876. The present building replaces two previous Academy structures, one by John Dorsey (1805–6) and the other by Richard A. Gilpin (1846–47).

References: Records of the Academy; *Exercises at the Laying of the Corner-Stone of the New Building for the Pennsylvania Academy of the Fine Arts,* Philadelphia, 1872; E[verett] S[hinn], "The First American Art Academy," *Lippincott's Magazine,* February–March 1872, pp. 143–153, 309–321; *Inauguration of the New Building of the Pennsylvania Academy,* 1876; *AABN:* I, March 4, 1876, p. 80; October 14, 1876, p. 335.

See plates 2 and 3

3-2 Window detail, Broad Street facade

3-3 Students' entrance, Cherry Street

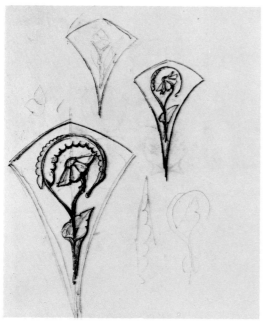

3-4 Ornament detail, above students' entrance. Sketchbook drawing. *c.* 1875. Collection George Wood Furness

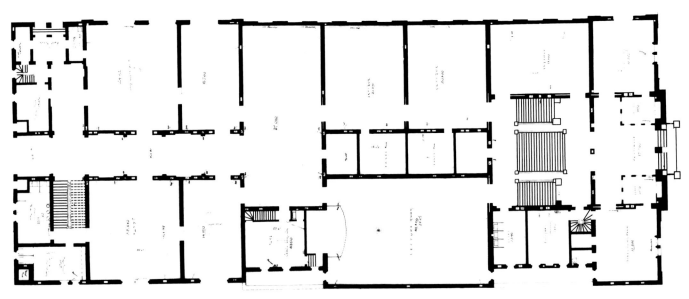

3-5 Furness and Hewitt. First-floor heating plan (preliminary).
Pennsylvania Academy of the Fine Arts, Philadelphia

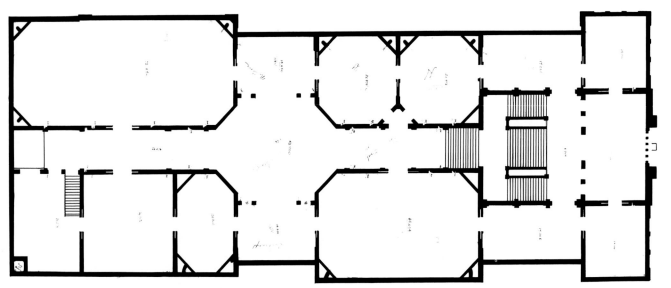

3-6 Furness and Hewitt. Gallery level heating plan (preliminary). Pennsylvania Academy of the Fine Arts, Philadelphia

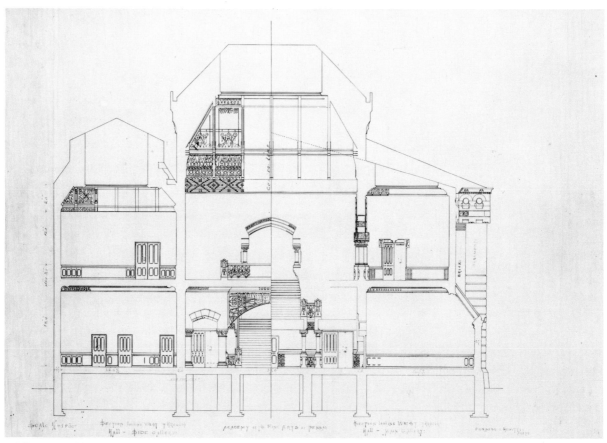

3-7 Furness and Hewitt. Transverse section looking west (preliminary). Pennsylvania Academy of the Fine Arts, Philadelphia

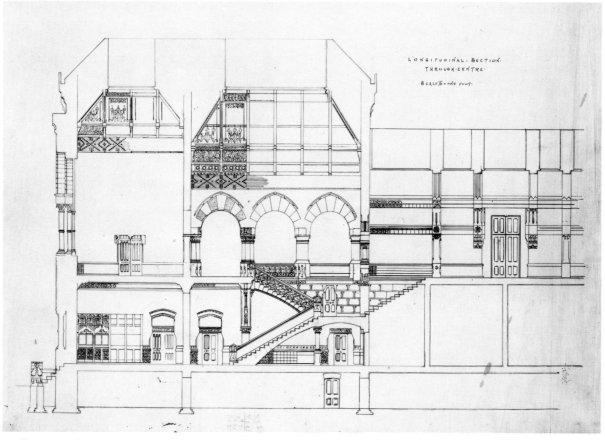

3-8 Furness and Hewitt. Longitudinal section looking south (preliminary). Pennsylvania Academy of the Fine Arts, Philadelphia

3-10 Stairhall

3-12 Painting gallery

3-11 Stairhall, detail

3-9 (opposite) Stairhall

3-13 Rear stair, detail

# 4 Jewish Hospital (now Einstein Medical Center)

**Broad Street and Old York Road**
**Furness and Hewitt; Furness and Evans;**
**Furness, Evans and Co.**

Commissions for the Jewish Hospital
Association, many of whose leaders were
members of the Rodef Shalom
congregation and the Mount Sinai
Cemetery Association, stretched over
Furness's whole career. Furness and
Hewitt's design for the main building was
accepted in December 1871, and the
structure was completed in 1873. The
Home for the Aged and Infirm Israelites
was added in 1888; a consumptives ward
in 1899; and the Guggenheim Wing, the
Loeb Operating Ward, and the Eisner
Home for Nurses in 1902. An isolating
ward was erected in 1903, and a sterilizing
room was finished in 1907. The last
survivor among these many Furness
buildings, the Home for the Aged, was
demolished in 1971.

References: *Ninth Annual Report of the Jewish
Hospital Association of Philadelphia,*
Philadelphia, 1874, pp. 48–51; *PRERBG,* III,
no. 2, January 16, 1888; *PI:* March 5, 1897,
p. 13; May 4, 1899, p. 9; February 25, 1902,
p. 6; March 29, 1902, p. 7; July 14, 1902, p.
13; August 6, 1902, p. 4; September 3, 1902,
p. 11; September 19, 1903, p. 15; March 21,
1905, p. 15; June 15, 1905, p. 9; *PRERBG,*
XXII, no. 43, October 23, 1907.

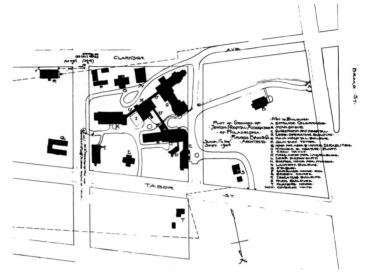

4-2 Furness, Evans and Co. Plot of grounds. 1904. Collection Einstein Medical
Center, Philadelphia

4-4 Furness, Evans and Co. The Home for the Aged and Infirm Israelites. Stair
detail. Courtesy Hyman Myers.

4-3 Furness, Evans and Co. The Home for the Aged and Infirm
Israelites. Exterior from northwest. Courtesy Lawrence S.
Williams, Inc., Philadelphia

4-1 (opposite) Furness, Evans and Co. The Home for the
Aged and Infirm Israelites. Northwest pavilion. Courtesy
Lawrence S. Williams, Inc., Philadelphia

4-5 Furness and Hewitt. Jewish Hospital. North façade.
Photo-zincograph. Collection Einstein Medical Center, Philadelphia

4-6 Furness, Evans and Co. Guggenheim Wing. Exterior
from southwest. Courtesy Einstein Medical Center, Philadelphia

## 5 Philadelphia Warehouse Company

### 235 Dock Street
### Furness and Hewitt

Despite its name, this now-demolished building was a bank. Probably designed and erected 1872–73.

References: *The Philadelphia Sketch-Club*, Philadelphia, 1874, Pl. 10; Philadelphia Contributionship Insurance Records (MS in Historical Society of Pennsylvania), 1899.

5–2 Exterior from southwest. Engraving (from *The Philadelphia Sketch-Club*, 1874). Free Library of Philadelphia

5–1 Exterior from southwest. Philadelphia Contributionship photograph. Historical Society of Pennsylvania, Philadelphia

## 6 Guarantee Trust and Safe Deposit Company

### 316–320 Chestnut Street
### Furness and Hewitt

A study for the façade appears in Furness's sketchbook dated 1873; the building was finished by 1875. Demolished 1956–57.

References: *AABN*, II, September 22, 1877, p. 308; [Pennsylvania Historical Society], *City of Philadelphia*, New York, 1886, p. 78; Massey 1, p. 13.

6-2 Exterior from northwest. Color lithograph by Bunk and McFetridge, Philadelphia. Historical Society of Pennsylvania, Philadelphia

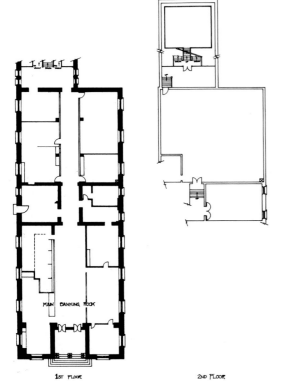

6-4 Plans of first and second floors. Redrawn by Marianna Thomas from twentieth-century plans

6-1 (opposite) Frank Furness. Study for Chestnut Street elevation. Sketchbook drawing. 1873. Collection George Wood Furness

6-3 Exterior from northeast. c. 1955. Courtesy James L. Dillon and Co., Inc., Philadelphia

6-5 Main banking room, detail of clerestory. Photograph by
Penelope Hartshorne. Courtesy Independence Hall National
Park, Philadelphia

6-6 Main banking room. Photograph by Penelope Hartshorne. Courtesy Independence Hall National Park, Philadelphia

6-7 Main banking room, teller's cage. Photograph by Penelope Hartshorne. Courtesy Independence Hall National Park, Philadelphia

6-8 Entrance door detail. Photograph by Penelope Hartshorne. Courtesy Independence Hall National Park, Philadelphia

6-9 Rear stair detail. Photograph by Penelope Hartshorne. Courtesy Independence Hall National Park, Philadelphia

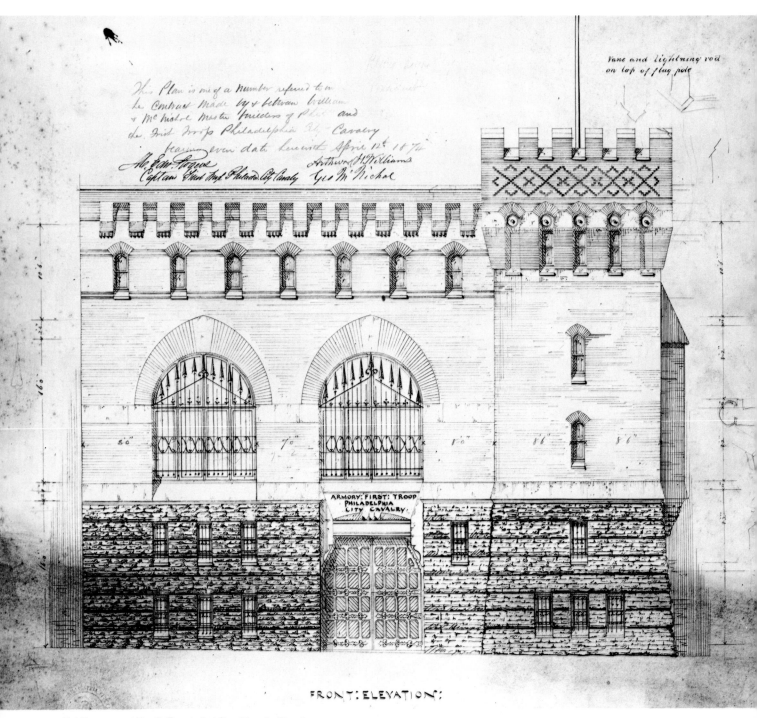

Vane and lightning rod
on top of flag pole

ARMORY: FIRST: TROOP
PHILADELPHIA
CITY CAVALRY

FRONT: ELEVATION:

7-1 Furness and Hewitt. Twenty-first Street façade. Elevation.
Collection First Troop, Philadelphia City Cavalry

## 7 Addition to the Armory for the First Troop, Philadelphia City Cavalry

**Twenty-first and Barker Streets**
**Furness and Hewitt**

Fraser, Furness and Hewitt were given a commission to extend the existing troop armory at Twenty-first and Barker streets in 1870. The specifications (in the archives of the Troop) provided for a green stone and red brick building. That commission was not executed; however, when in 1874 it was decided to enlarge the building, Furness and Hewitt were called upon to do the addition. The cornerstone was laid July 4, 1874, and the building was dedicated in November of the same year. It partially collapsed and was demolished in 1899.

References: *History of the First Troop, Philadelphia City Cavalry,* Philadelphia, 1875; *AABN,* I, October 14, 1876, p. 335; *PI,* March 6, 1899, p. 10; Massey 1, pp. 15–16.

7-2 Exterior from northeast. Courtesy First Troop, Philadelphia City Cavalry

## 8 Addition to the Pennsylvania Institution for the Deaf and Dumb (now Philadelphia College of Art)

**Broad and Pine Streets**
**Furness and Hewitt**

The commission for this brick addition, which more than doubled the size of John Haviland's original building of 1824, was awarded in December 1874, and the addition was finished the following year.

Reference: *The Annual Report of the Board of Directors of the Pennsylvania Institution for the Deaf and Dumb for the Year 1875,* Philadelphia, 1876, p. 7.

8-2 Exterior from south

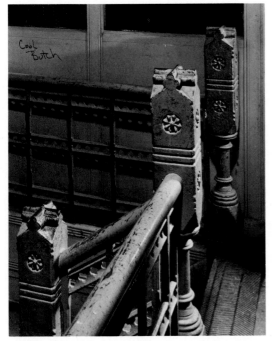
8-4 Iron stair detail

8-3 Exterior from west

8-1 (opposite) Exterior detail from south, chimney

## 9 Thomas Hockley House

**235 South Twenty-first Street
Furness and Hewitt**

Probably 1875; Hockley was living in the
house by 1876. Altered and added to in
1894 by Furness, Evans and Co. It is
now divided into apartments.
Other commissions associated with
Hockley include the Armory, First City
Troop, and the Reliance Insurance
Company, of which he was an officer.

References: *Gopsill's Philadelphia City
Directory,* 1876; *Philadelphia Press,* July 5,
1885, p. 12; *PRERBG,* IX, no. 38, September
19, 1894; Massey 1, p. 16.

See plate 4

9–2 Entrance porch and chimney detail

9–3 Front door

9–1 (opposite) Exterior from west

10-1 Main facade (from *AABN*, I, September 9, 1876)

## 10 Jefferson Medical College Hospital

### Tenth and Sansom Streets
### Furness and Hewitt

The building replaced a porticoed classical structure designed by Napoleon LeBrun. The commission, won in competition with three other architects (one of whom was Thomas W. Richards), was awarded in September 1875, and the contracts let in November. The hospital was finished by 1877, when a second building by Furness and Hewitt was under construction. Both were demolished in 1922.

References: Records of Thomas Jefferson University; AABN: I, September 9, 1876, p. 292; II, August 25, 1877, p. 273.

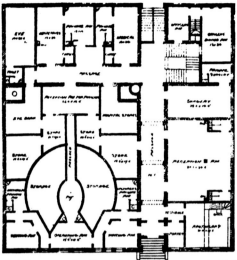

10-2 First-story plan (from AABN, I, September 9, 1876)

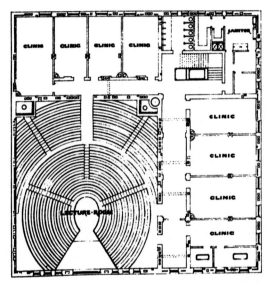

10-3 Second-story plan (from AABN, I, September 9, 1876)

10-5 Exterior. Courtesy Thomas Jefferson University, Philadelphia

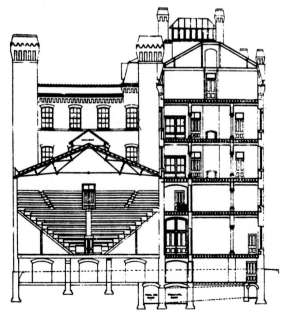

10-4 Section, through lecture room (from AABN, I, September 9, 1876)

11-1 Elephant House. Woodcut (from *Fifth Annual Report . . .* , 1877)

## 11 Philadelphia Zoological Gardens

### Thirty-fourth Street and Girard Avenue
### Furness and Hewitt

The Elephant House was erected in the summer of 1875, and the Restaurant was open by March 1876. Preliminary studies for both are in one of Furness's sketchbooks. Hewitt designed the Antelope House and the Aviary and is credited with the gatehouses, although Furness probably had a hand in their design. Other buildings of this period at the Zoo were by Collins and Autenrieth (Carnivore House) and Theophilus P. Chandler (Bear Pits). Of Furness and Hewitt's work only the gatehouses survive.

References: *Third Annual Report of the Board of Managers of the Zoological Society of Philadelphia,* Philadelphia, 1875, pp. 10–11; *Fourth Annual Report . . .,* 1876, pp. 8–10; *Fifth Annual Report . . .,* 1877, p. 9; *AABN,* II, January 6, 1877, p. 7; *Scientific American:* XXXIX, August 3, 1878, p. 71; XXXIX, October 5, 1878, pp. 214–215.

11-2 Frank Furness. Preliminary studies for Elephant House. Elevation and section. Sketchbook drawing. Collection George Wood Furness

11-3 Frank Furness. Preliminary study for Elephant House. Elevation. Sketchbook drawing. Collection George Wood Furness

11-4 Elephant House. Exterior, general view. Courtesy Philadelphia Zoological Society

103

11-5 Gatehouses. Woodcut (from *Fifth Annual Report* . . . ,
1877)

11-6 Restaurant. Woodcut (from *Fifth Annual Report* . . . ,
1877)

11-7 Gatehouse detail

11-8 Frank Furness. Preliminary studies for Zoo Restaurant. Sketchbook drawing. Collection George Wood Furness

12-1 Overall view. Engraving. Collection George E. Thomas

## 12 Brazilian Pavilion

### Main Building, Centennial Exhibition
### Frank Furness

Erected for the Centennial Exhibition of 1876 and presumably destroyed at its close.

References: *AABN,* I, May 13, 1876, p. 160; James D. McCabe, *The Illustrated History of the Centennial Exhibition,* Philadelphia, 1876, pp. 453–457; *Scientific American Supplement,* I, June 17, 1876, p. 385.

12-2 Interior of Exhibition. Courtesy Hyman Myers

12-3 "The Brazilian and Netherlands Departments," Main Building, Centennial Exhibition. Engraving (from *Frank Leslie's Historical Register of the United States Centennial Exposition,* 1876)

108

## 13 Centennial National Bank (now First Pennsylvania Bank)

**Thirty-second and Market Streets**
**Frank Furness**

Erected in 1876; the one-story wing to the south was given an adjacent, identical extension, and the interior was altered, both in 1899 by Frank Miles Day. There have been recent extensive alterations; windows and roof lines have been simplified.

References: *AABN,* I, December 23, 1876, p. 414; *PI,* May 15, 1899, p. 10.

13-2 Exterior from northwest

13-3 Frank Furness. Study for the elevation of a bank. Sketchbook drawing. Collection George Wood Furness

13-4 Frank Furness. Study for the elevation of a bank. Sketchbook drawing. Collection George Wood Furness

13-1 (opposite) Exterior from north

110

## 14  The Provident Life and Trust Company

### 409 Chestnut Street and later additions
### Frank Furness; Furness, Evans and Co.

Furness won the commission for 409 Chestnut in the summer of 1876 in competition with George Hewitt, James H. Windrim, and Addison Hutton (architect of the Provident's second building of 1872). The result was an L-shaped building fronting on Chestnut and on Fourth streets. 409 Chestnut was not finished until 1879 because of a two-year delay due to a business crisis. In 1888 Furness won a second competition for a ten-story addition to stretch from the first building to the corner of Fourth and Chestnut. His competitors included such diverse architects as William Ralph Emerson of Boston, George C. Mason of Newport, and George T. Pearson of Philadelphia. The building was under roof in 1889 and finished in 1890. Later additions by Furness, Evans and Co. extended the building northward on Fourth to Ranstead Street. All have been demolished.

References: "Minutes of the Board of Directors of the Provident Life and Trust Company" (MS), meetings of August 7, 1876, and February 13, 1888; *PI:* February 11, 1892, p. 7; June 4, 1902, p. 7; William Ashbrook, *The Provident Life and Trust Company of Philadelphia, 1865–1915*, Philadelphia, 1915; J. C. Massey, "The Provident Trust Buildings," *JSAH*, XIX, May 1960, pp. 79–81.

14-2 Frank Furness. 409 Chestnut Street. Main façade. *c.* 1885. Photograph by Tremaine's Architectural Photographers. Courtesy Historical Society of Pennsylvania, Philadelphia. Penrose Collection

14-1 (opposite) William M. Camac, for Frank Furness. 409 Chestnut Street. Main façade. 1876–77. Engraving (from *Insurance Blue Book, 1876–1877*)

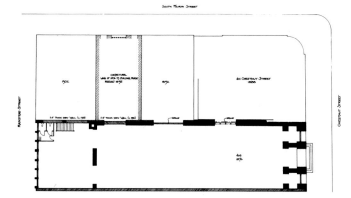

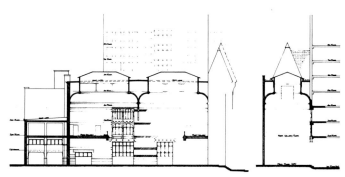

14-3 Frank Furness. Plan, showing 409 Chestnut Street with ell to Fourth Street. Redrawn by Marianna Thomas from plan of George W. Casey and Herman E. Kleinfelder (c. 1931)

14-4 Frank Furness. Longitudinal and transverse sections. Redrawn by Marianna Thomas from plan of George W. Casey and Herman E. Kleinfelder (c. 1931)

14-5 Frank Furness. Fourth Street elevation (from *The Baxter Panoramic Business Directory*, May 1879)

14-6 (opposite) Frank Furness and Furness, Evans and Co. 401-409 Chestnut Street with additions. After 1902. Courtesy Free Library of Philadelphia

112

14-7 Frank Furness. 409 Chestnut Street. Main banking room looking south. Courtesy Independence Hall National Park, Philadelphia

14-8 Frank Furness. 409 Chestnut Street. Main banking room looking north. Before 1912. Photo-engraving. Collection Provident Mutual Life Insurance Company, Philadelphia

14-10 Furness, Evans and Co. 401 Chestnut Street. Interior. Before 1912. Photo-engraving. Collection Provident Mutual Life Insurance Company, Philadelphia

14-9 Frank Furness. 409 Chestnut Street. Main banking room looking north. Before 1912. Photo-engraving. Collection Provident Mutual Life Insurance Company, Philadelphia

14-11 Furness, Evans and Co. 401 Chestnut Street. Teller's cage detail. Before 1912. Photo-engraving. Collection Provident Mutual Life Insurance Company, Philadelphia

## Kensington National Bank (now First Pennsylvania Bank)

### Frankford and Girard Avenues
### Frank Furness

The *American Architect* of August 25, 1877, describes this as a new building; Holdsworth also dates it 1877. The building has been extended to the west, the skyline simplified, and the interior completely altered.

References: *AABN,* II, August 25, 1877, p. 273; J. T. Holdsworth, *History of Banking in Philadelphia,* Philadelphia, 1928, IV, p. 382.

15-2 Exterior from northeast

15-3 Exterior, window

15-1 (opposite) Exterior from northeast. c. 1880. Courtesy Historical Society of Pennsylvania, Philadelphia

16-1 Exterior from southeast

## 16 Church of the Redeemer for Seamen and Their Families and Charles Brewer School

**Front and Queen Streets**
**Frank Furness**

Cornerstone laid in June 1878. The building was consecrated in January 1879. Church destroyed by fire in 1974.

References: "Records of the Board of Managers, Churchmen's Missionary Association for Seamen of the Port of Philadelphia" (MS), meeting of September 10, 1878; Massey 1, p. 16.

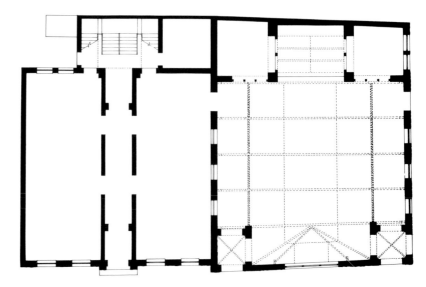

16-2 Plan of church and school. Drawn by Hugh McCauley

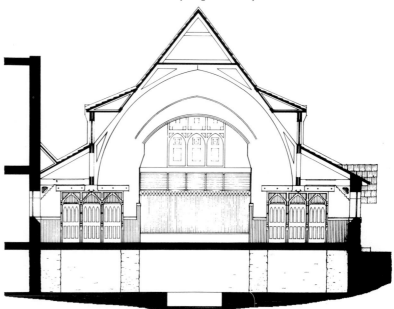

16-3 Transverse section of church. Drawn by Hugh McCauley

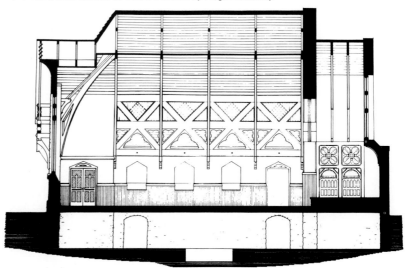

16-4 Longitudinal section of church. Drawn by Hugh McCauley

16-6 Queen Street façade. School entrance at left

16-7 Queen Street façade, detail. Photograph by Jack Boucher. Courtesy *HABS*. Library of Congress, Washington, D.C.

16-5 (opposite) Interior of church

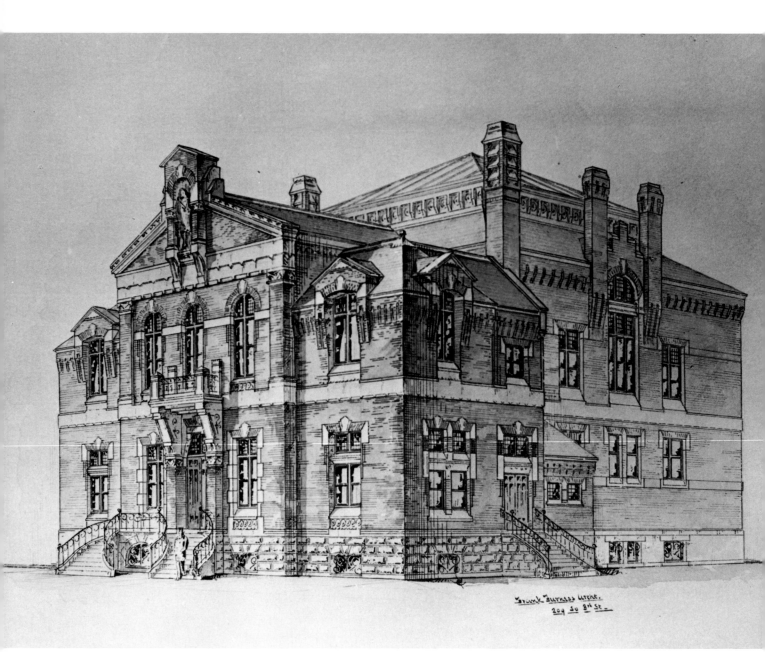

17-1 Frank Furness. Exterior from southeast. Colored ink
drawing. Library Company of Philadelphia

## 17  Library Company of Philadelphia

**Locust and Juniper Streets**
**Frank Furness**

Furness and his competitors, Addison Hutton, Collins and Autenrieth, James C. Sidney, and Theophilus P. Chandler, submitted proposals for a fireproof library to the board of directors on January 20, 1879. Furness, who in his design had "endeavored to suggest the lines of the present building" (that is, William Thornton's library of 1789), won the commission. The building was opened in February 1880. Extended by Collins and Autenrieth in 1888, and demolished in 1940.

References: "Minutes of the Board of Directors, Library Company of Philadelphia" (MS), 1875–1885, pp. 190–200; *Public Ledger,* February 20, 1879, p. 3; *Pl,* May 9, 1888, p. 6; Tatum, p. 195.

17-2 Reading room. Courtesy Library Company of Philadelphia

17-3 Reading room. Courtesy Library Company of Philadelphia

18-1 Exterior from southwest

## 18 William H. Rhawn House: "Knowlton"

### 8001 Verree Road, Fox Chase
### Frank Furness

William H. Rhawn, one of Furness's most important early patrons, was an officer of the Guarantee Trust Company in 1872 and president of the National Bank of the Republic in 1884. "Knowlton" was probably designed in 1879 and finished in 1881 (the date in the glass of the entry). The rooms to the north of the eastern range are clearly a later addition. The stables and caretaker's house are extant.

Reference: *AABN*, VII, February 28, 1880, p. 88.

See plates 5 and 6

18-2 Stables. Exterior from west

18-3 Exterior from east

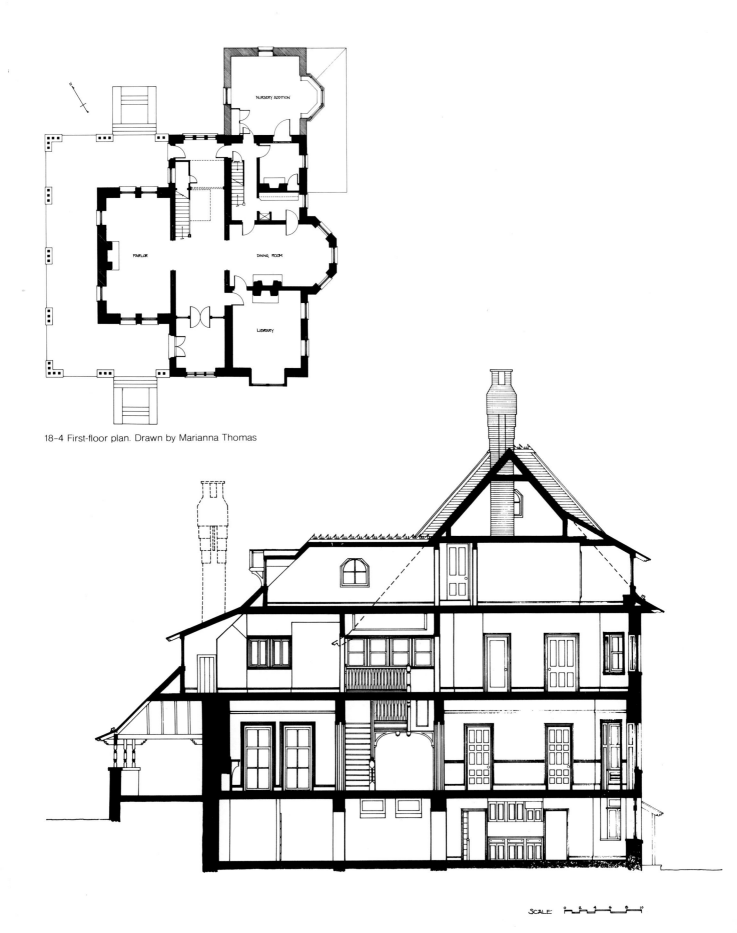

18-4 First-floor plan. Drawn by Marianna Thomas

18-5 Section. Drawn by Marianna Thomas

18-6 Entrance hall, from stairhall

18-7 Stairhall, from dining room

18-8 Stair newel

18-9 Dining room

18-11 Library

18-12 Second-floor bedroom

18-13 Second-floor bedroom, fireplace detail

18-10 (opposite) Entrance hall detail

## 9 Philadelphia and Reading Railroad Depot

**Graver's Lane, Chestnut Hill**
**Frank Furness**

Designed prior to 1884, when Furness ceased working for the Reading, according to his letter of December 23, 1884, to John E. Wooten, general manager of the railroad, in the Historical Society of Pennsylvania. A signed drawing for the depot is in the archives of the Philadelphia and Reading Railroad Company.

Reference: unpublished?

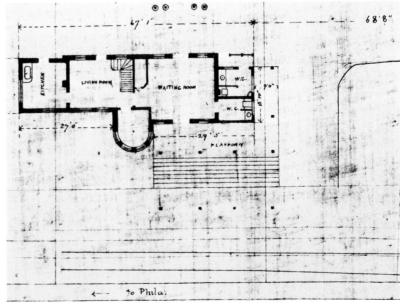

19-2 Plan, after Frank Furness, from signed original in Collection of Philadelphia and Reading Railroad Company

19-3 Trackside elevation

19-1 (opposite) Porte-cochere from northwest

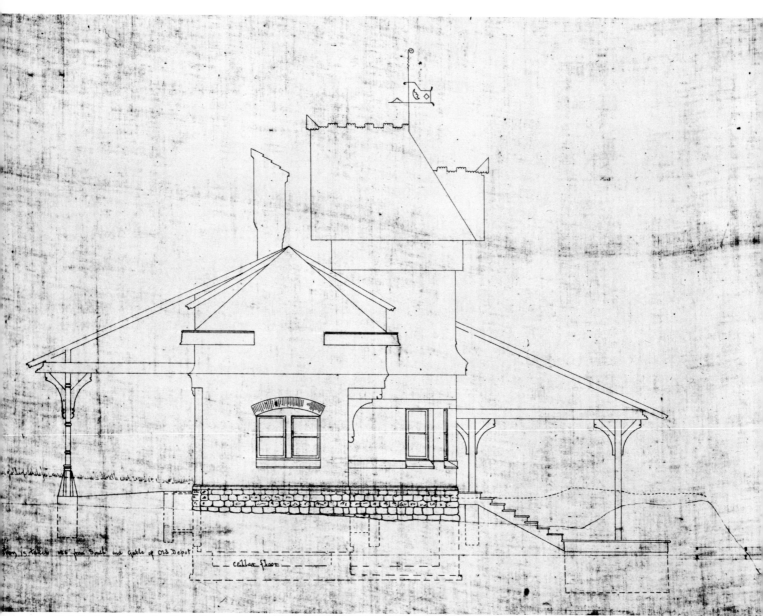

19-4 South elevation, after Frank Furness, from original in
Collection of Philadelphia and Reading Railroad Company

19-5 Tower detail

19-6 Porte-cochere from west

19-7 Porte-cochere detail

19-8 Exterior from northwest

20-1 Exterior from southwest

## 20 Clement Griscom House: "Dolobran"

**Haverford, Pennsylvania**
**Furness and Evans; Furness, Evans and Co.**

An earlier farm house was remodeled and extended about 1881 (the date on an initialed terra-cotta plaque on the south side of the house). This work is attributed to Furness not only on the basis of style, but also because Furness added to the house in 1894 and, with Karl Bitter, designed the interiors of two steamships for Griscom's American Line: the *St. Paul* and the *St. Louis.* The exterior surfaces have been changed.

References: *PRERBG*, IX, no. 35, August 29, 1894; *Scientific American,* LXXII, June 15, 1895, p. 376.

20-2 Second-floor bedroom, fireplace

20-3 First-floor alcove, fireplace

20-4 Stairhall

20-5 Leaded-glass window

## 21 Penn National Bank

**Seventh and Market Streets**
**Furness and Evans**

The Penn National Bank was designed in 1882 and the building was completed by the fall of 1884; it was demolished in the 1930s. The bank's president, Gillies Dallett, was the great-uncle of E. James Dallett, who was at that time a draftsman in Furness's office. The key document is a photograph, in the Penrose Collection of the Historical Society of Pennsylvania, of the National Bank of the Republic, which lists on the back photographs by the Pittsburgh-based firm, Tremaine's Architectural Photographers, of three buildings by Furness, including the Penn National Bank.

Reference: William Campbell, "Frank Furness, An American Pioneer," *Architectural Review*, CX, no. 659, November 1951, pp. 311 ff.

21-2 Exterior from northeast. Photograph by Tremaine's Architectural Photographers. Courtesy Historical Society of Pennsylvania, Philadelphia. Penrose Collection

21-1 (opposite) Banking room. c. 1890. Courtesy Historical Society of Pennsylvania, Philadelphia

22-1 Water tower from north

## 22 Samuel Shipley House: "Winden"

**West Chester, Pennsylvania**
**Furness and Evans**

An Italianate stone house of 1857 (datestone on south side of the house) was enlarged in 1882 (plaque on south side of library wing). The additions are attributed to Furness on the basis of style, and because of the continuing stream of commissions Furness received from Shipley, including the various Provident bank buildings and a later house, "Town's End," also in West Chester. In a recent conversation Mrs. Page Allinson, Shipley's daughter, confirmed the attribution to Furness.

Reference: Massey 2, p. 26.

22-2 Exterior of farmhouse from south. Before 1882. Courtesy Mr. and Mrs. Alexander Phillips

22-3 Exterior from south

22-5 Second-floor bedroom, fireplace

22-4 Exterior from northeast

22-7 Exterior from east

22-6 (opposite) Exterior from northwest

23-1 Exterior from west

## 23 Undine Barge Club

### East River Drive
### Furness and Evans

Designed and erected 1882–83. There
have been some minor changes on the
river side.

Reference: Louis Heiland, *The Undine Barge
Club of Philadelphia,* Philadelphia, 1925.

See plate 7

23-2 Exterior from east

23-3 Exterior from river

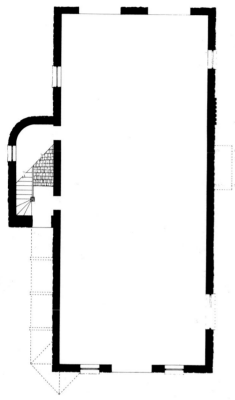

23-5 First-floor plan. Drawn by Hugh McCauley

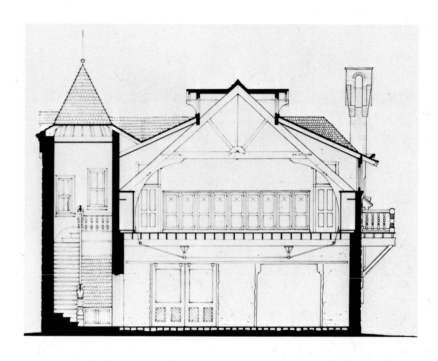

23-6 Transverse section. Drawn by Hugh McCauley

23-7 Clubroom, fireplace detail

23-8 Second-floor locker room

23-4 (opposite) Interior, stairway

## 24 First Unitarian Church and Parish House

**Chestnut and Van Pelt Streets**
**Furness and Evans**

The Furness family church included among its members many of Furness's clients, including Mrs. Samuel Shipley. The new building, designed in 1883, replaced an earlier church by William Strickland, which was itself a replacement for Robert Mills's Octagonal Church of 1812. The cornerstone was laid in 1885 and the church dedicated in 1886. The Parish House was finished by 1884. The church and parish house were altered in 1902 and later.

References: *The Laying of the Cornerstone of the Third Church Edifice of the First Unitarian Society of Philadelphia,* Philadelphia, 1885, p. 10; *PRERBG,* I, no. 6, February 15, 1886; *PI,* April 26, 1902, p. 7.

24-2 Exterior from southeast. Before 1900. Courtesy First Unitarian Church, Philadelphia

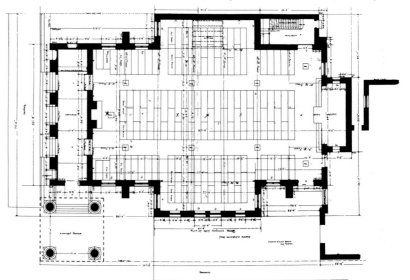
24-3 Plan, after Furness and Evans. Collection First Unitarian Church, Philadelphia

24-4 Exterior from southeast

24-1 (opposite) Nave, looking toward entrance

24-5 Exterior, detail of original stonework

24-6 Reading desk

24-7 Nave, facing chancel. Courtesy James L. Dillon and Co., Inc., Philadelphia

24-8 Parish House. Chimney detail

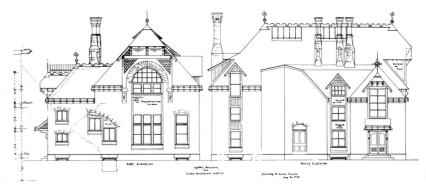

24-9 Parish House. East and south elevation, after Furness and Evans. Collection First Unitarian Church, Philadelphia

24-10 (opposite) Parish House. Second-floor fireplace

## 25 National Bank of the Republic
### (later Philadelphia Clearing House)

**313 Chestnut Street**
**Furness and Evans**

Building permits were issued in January 1884, suggesting 1883 as the year of the commission. William H. Rhawn was the president of the bank. The building was sold to the Philadelphia Clearing House and altered by Furness, Evans and Co. in 1904. Demolished 1953.

References: *AABN,* XV, January 26, 1884, p. 48; *PRERBG,* XIX, no. 10, March 1904; Lee Nelson, "White, Furness, McNally and the Capital National Bank of Salem, Oregon," *JSAH,* XIX, May 1960, pp. 57 ff.

25-2 300 block, north side, Chestnut Street, showing from left, John McArthur's First National Bank, Furness and Evans's National Bank of the Republic, and John T. Windrim's Bank of North America. Courtesy Free Library of Philadelphia

25-4 Ornament detail above fireplace at north end of banking room. 1955. Courtesy William Campbell

25-1 (opposite) Street façade. Before 1893. Courtesy Historical Society of Pennsylvania, Philadelphia

25-3 Main banking room looking north. Before 1890. Courtesy Historical Society of Pennsylvania, Philadelphia

26-1 Chestnut Street looking east. *c.* 1925. Courtesy Historical Society of Pennsylvania, Philadelphia

## 26 Baltimore and Ohio Passenger Station

**Twenty-fourth and Chestnut Streets**
**Furness, Evans and Co.**
**(the drawings signed "Frank Furness Archt.")**

Designed in 1886 and largely completed
by 1888, this station was demolished
about 1963. The drawings are in the
Historical Society of Pennsylvania.

References: *PRERBG*, I, no. 32, August 16,
1886; Massey 2, p. 29.

26-2 Exterior from northeast. c. 1890. Engraving. Free Library of Philadelphia

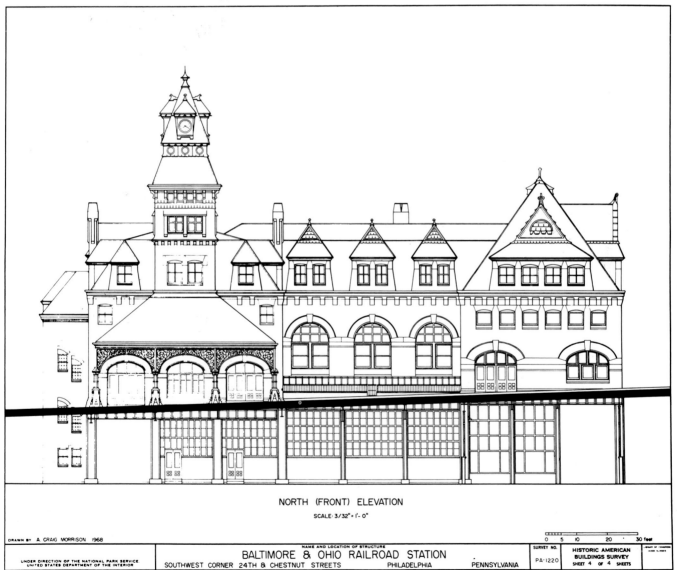

NORTH (FRONT) ELEVATION

SCALE: 3/32" = 1'-0"

DRAWN BY A. CRAIG MORRISON 1968

UNDER DIRECTION OF THE NATIONAL PARK SERVICE.
UNITED STATES DEPARTMENT OF THE INTERIOR

| NAME AND LOCATION OF STRUCTURE | SURVEY NO. | HISTORIC AMERICAN |
|---|---|---|
| BALTIMORE & OHIO RAILROAD STATION | PA-1220 | BUILDINGS SURVEY |
| SOUTHWEST CORNER 24TH & CHESTNUT STREETS      PHILADELPHIA      PENNSYLVANIA | | SHEET 4 OF 4 SHEETS |

0  5  10      20      30 feet

26-3 North elevation. Drawing, 1968, by A. Craig Morrison for *HABS*, after drawings by Frank
Furness in the Historical Society of Pennsylvania. Library of Congress, Washington, D.C.

26-4 (opposite) Exterior from west. Courtesy Baltimore and Ohio Railroad Company, Baltimore

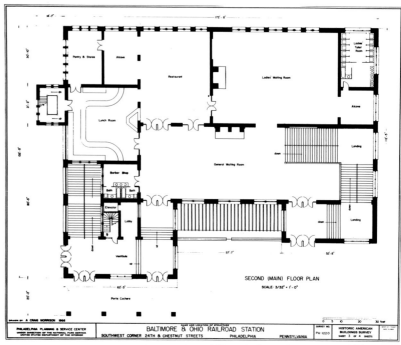

26-6 Second (main) floor plan. After drawing, 1966, by A. Craig Morrison for *HABS*. Library of Congress, Washington, D.C.

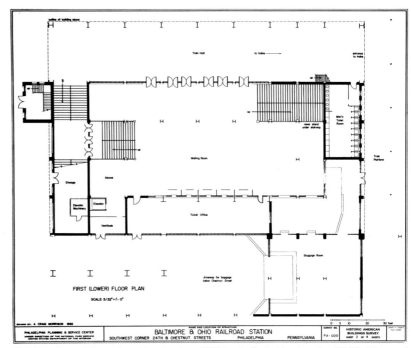

26-7 First (lower) floor plan. After drawing, 1966, by A. Craig Morrison for *HABS*. Library of Congress, Washington, D.C.

26-5 (opposite) Exterior from east. Courtesy Baltimore and Ohio Railroad Company, Baltimore

26-9 Interior, main stair. Courtesy Historical Society of Pennsylvania, Philadelphia

26-10 General waiting room, fireplace. Photograph by Cervin Robinson. Courtesy *HABS*. Library of Congress, Washington, D.C.

26-8 (opposite) Interior, stair detail. Photograph by Cervin Robinson. Courtesy *HABS*. Library of Congress, Washington, D.C.

26-11 General waiting room, fireplace detail. Photograph by Cervin Robinson. Courtesy *HABS*. Library of Congress, Washington, D.C.

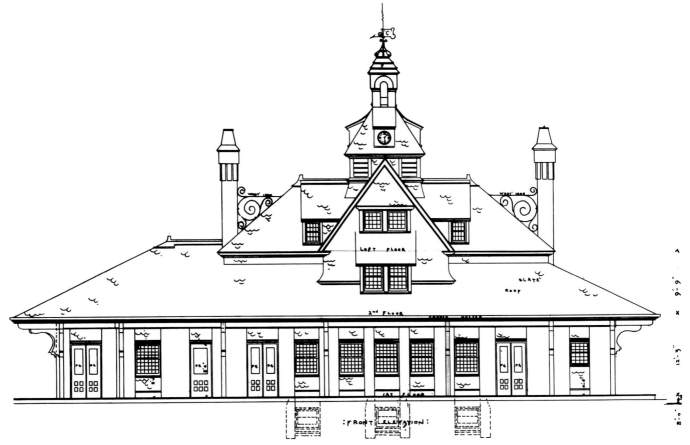

27-1 Frank Furness. Front elevation. May 1886. Historical
Society of Pennsylvania, Philadelphia

27-2 Frank Furness. Rear elevation. May 1886. Historical
Society of Pennsylvania, Philadelphia

## 27 Baltimore and Ohio Railroad Depot

**Chester, Pennsylvania**
**Furness, Evans and Co.**
**(the drawings signed "Frank Furness:**
**Architect")**

Working drawings for this demolished
station are in the Historical Society of
Pennsylvania. They are dated 1886.

Reference: Massey 2, p. 29.

27-3 General view. Courtesy Baltimore and Ohio Railroad Company, Baltimore

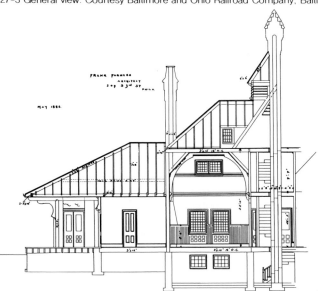

27-4 Frank Furness. Section through Women's Waiting Room and Express Office. May 1886. Historical Society of Pennsylvania, Philadelphia

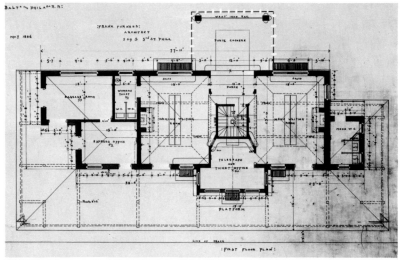

27-5 Frank Furness. First-floor plan. May 1886. Historical Society of Pennsylvania, Philadelphia

28-1 Stairhall

## 28 William Winsor House: "Hedgely"

**Ardmore, Pennsylvania**
**Furness, Evans and Co.**

Furness's alterations and additions to this old farm house can be dated 1887 by the surviving blueprints. William Winsor was the father-in-law of Horace Howard Furness, Jr. The building has been simplified considerably in recent years.

Reference: unpublished?

28-2 Furness, Evans and Co. Side elevation. Private collection

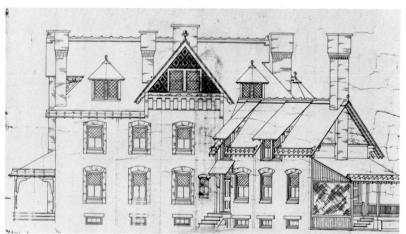

28-3 Furness, Evans and Co. Rear elevation. Private collection

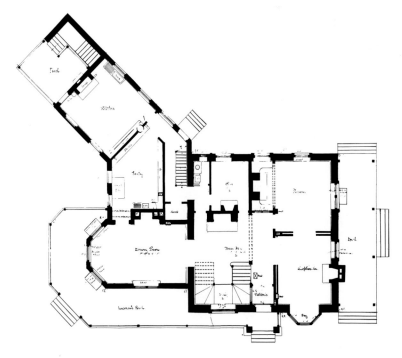

28-4 Furness, Evans and Co. First-floor plan. Private collection

28-5 Parlor, detail of fireback

28-6 Upstairs bedroom, fireplace detail

28-7 Main stairhall, detail of fireback

28-8 Main stairhall, fireplace

## 29  Library, University of Pennsylvania (now Furness Building)

**Thirty-fourth Street between Spruce and Walnut Streets**
**Furness, Evans and Co.**

Embarrassed by the fact that it was the last "great seat of learning in the country which had no library," the university decided in 1887 to erect such a building. The committee, chaired by Horace Howard Furness, selected Furness, Evans and Co. as the architects. The cornerstone was laid in October 1888, and the building was opened in February 1891. Additions include the Duhring Wing (Furness, Evans and Co., 1914–15), the Lea Library and Reading Room (Furness, Evans and Co., 1924), and the Horace Howard Furness Memorial Library (Robert McGoodwin, 1931).

References: *PI,* June 20, 1888, p. 2; *PRERBG,* III, no. 28, July 16, 1888; T. Williams, "Plans for the Library of the University of Pennsylvania," *Library Journal,* XIII, August 1888, pp. 237–243; *Proceedings of the Opening of the Library of the University of Pennsylvania,* Philadelphia, 1891; M. Schuyler, "The Architecture of American Colleges," *Architectural Record,* XXVIII, September 1910, pp. 187–191.

See plate 8

29-2 View from southwest. Before 1914. Courtesy University of Pennsylvania, Philadelphia

29-3 View from southeast. Before 1914. Courtesy University of Pennsylvania, Philadelphia

29-4 View from north, with Thomas W. Richard's College Hall (1871). Before 1914. Courtesy University of Pennsylvania, Philadelphia

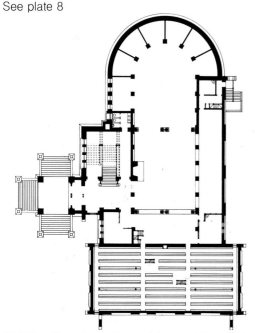
29-5 Plan. Drawn by David Stupplebeen and Hyman Myers

29-1 (opposite) Exterior from west

29-6 Joseph Huston of Furness, Evans and Co. Perspective from northwest, with projected extended stack. 1888. Ink drawing. Collection University of Pennsylvania, Philadelphia

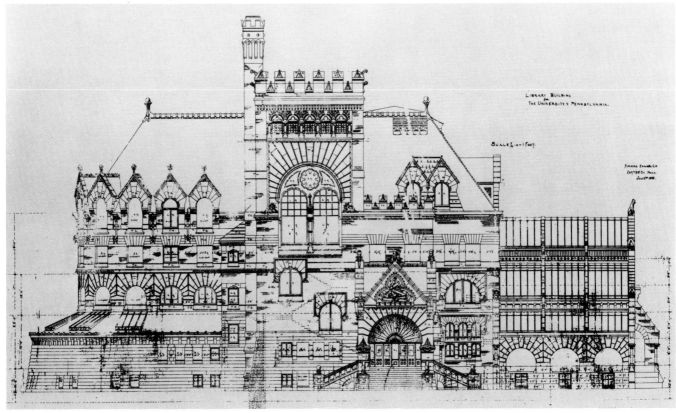

29-7 Furness, Evans and Co. Elevation of west façade as built. July 1888. Collection University of Pennsylvania, Philadelphia

29-8 Entrance porch detail

29-9 Exterior detail from west

29-11 Stair tower, detail of iron brackets

29-12 Main stair detail

29-13 Furness, Evans and Co. Section through entrance hall and stair tower. July 1888. Collection University of Pennsylvania, Philadelphia

29-10 (opposite) Stair tower, in use as University Museum. Before 1898. Courtesy University of Pennsylvania, Philadelphia

29-14 Stair tower detail

29-15 Leaded-glass window

29-16 Main reading room, detail of cusped brackets supporting skylight

29-17 "Rotunda" from main reading room

29-18 Main reading room. Before 1898. Courtesy University
of Pennsylvania, Philadelphia

## 30 Williamson Free School of Mechanical Trades

**Middletown Road, Elwyn, Pennsylvania**
**Furness, Evans and Co.**

Furness won this commission in 1889 in competition with Cope and Stewardson, George and William Hewitt, Thomas Lonsdale, and Wilson Brothers. The school was completed in 1891. Some of the buildings now on the grounds postdate Furness's work.

References: *Pl,* August 24, 1889, p. 3; *Builder, Decorator and Woodworker,* XIV, March 1, 1889, n.p.

See plate 9

30-3 Chapel interior. 1895. Courtesy Williamson Free School, Elwyn

30-2 Main building from south

30-1 (opposite) Main building, detail

30–4 Main building, entrance hall fireplace

30–5 Main building, stair

30-6 Shop building. Courtesy Williamson Free School, Elwyn

30-7 Powerhouse stack

30-8 Student residence from east

31-1 Exterior from west

31-2 Exterior from southeast

## 31  Bryn Mawr Hotel (now Baldwin School)

**Bryn Mawr, Pennsylvania**
**Furness, Evans and Co.**

The present building of 1890 replaced
a hotel designed by Wilson Brothers that
burned in the winter of 1889-90.  The
Pennsylvania Railroad was the client.
With vacationers turning to the seashore,
the hotel was sold within the decade
to the Baldwin School.

References: *PI*, January 26, 1890, p. 7;
Massey 3, p. 11.

See plate 10

31-3 Entrance hall

31-4 Lobby fireplace

31-5 Main stair

32-1 Exterior from southwest

## 32 Chapel, Mount Sinai Cemetery

**Bridge and Cottage Streets, Frankford**
**Furness, Evans and Co.**

Designed for the Mount Sinai Cemetery Association in 1891 and finished in February 1892.

Furness-designed buildings housed the major events of life in the Philadelphia Jewish community, from birth at the Jewish Hospital, through life's ceremonies at Rodef Shalom, to final rites at Mount Sinai Chapel.

References: *Pl,* February 27, 1892, p. 7; Massey 3, p. 11.

32-2 Exterior from northwest

32-3 Exterior from northeast

32-4 Interior

33-1 Market Street façade of train shed. Arch through viaduct. March 1903. Courtesy Historical Society of Pennsylvania, Philadelphia

## 33 Pennsylvania Railroad Station

**Broad and Market Streets**
**Furness, Evans and Co.**

Bids were received for Furness's addition to the Wilson Brothers' station (1881–82) in August of 1892. Work on the building was largely completed by the end of 1893. During the following year Furness's office added to and altered the upper levels of the Wilson Brothers' building. The terminal was demolished in 1952. The building was distinguished by several remarkable features, including the important terra-cotta reliefs by Karl Bitter, the immense train shed, and the great viaduct which joined the terminal to the yards at Thirtieth Street. The reliefs ornamented the headhouse and the train-shed wall; various panels presented the growth of the transportation industry and allegorically described the terminal cities of the Pennsylvania transportation empire. They defined the building as the architectural symbol of a national institution. The train shed, which had been the largest in the world, burned in 1923, but the viaduct remained to become a part of Philadelphia folklore. Its nickname "The Chinese Wall" expressed both its size and its impact on the city.

References: *PRERBG,* VII, no. 30, July 27, 1892; *PI:* August 31, 1892, p. 8; February 23, 1894, p. 6; Walter Berg, *Buildings and Structures of American Railroads,* New York, 1892, pp. 444-446; C. L. V. Meeks, *The Railroad Station,* New Haven, 1956, p. 88; Massey 3, pp. 9-10; James Dennis, *Karl Bitter,* Madison, Wis., 1967, pp. 56-63.

33-2 Perspective from southeast. Collection George E. Thomas

33-3 View from northeast. Courtesy James L. Dillon and Co., Inc., Philadelphia

33-4 Market Street façade of train shed, with headhouse building to right and tower of City Hall beyond. March 1903. Courtesy Historical Society of Pennsylvania, Philadelphia

33-5 Waiting room (from Edwin P. Alexander, *Down at the Depot,* 1970)

33-6 Karl Bitter. *Spirit of Transportation.* Terra-cotta relief. Main waiting room. Before 1900. Courtesy James L. Dillon and Co., Inc., Philadelphia

33-7 Train shed from west with headhouse and tower of City Hall beyond. Courtesy Harrison Albrecht

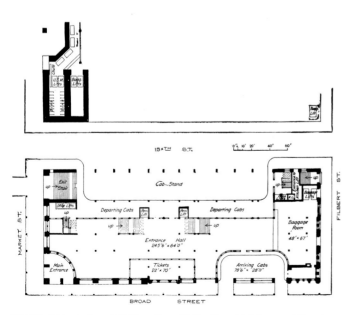

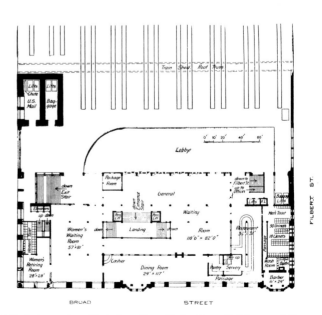

33-8 Preliminary plan of first floor (from Walter Berg, *Buildings and Structures of American Railroads,* 1892)

33-9 Preliminary plan of train floor (from Walter Berg, *Buildings and Structures of American Railroads,* 1892)

34-1 Exterior from east

## 34 Merion Cricket Club

**Montgomery Avenue, Haverford, Pennsylvania**
**Furness, Evans and Co.**

The clubhouse designed by the firm in 1892 was destroyed by fire in 1895. The firm designed a replacement but it too burned, in September 1896, just before its scheduled completion. The present structure is a rebuilding of the second clubhouse plus additions of 1905 and 1911. Members of the club included many of Furness's most important associates—Allen Evans and his brother Rowland, Clement Griscom, and Alexander J. Cassatt.

References: *Pl:* November 24, 1892, p. 2; November 2, 1895, p. 8; *PRERBG:* XI, no. 3, January 15, 1896; XI, no. 40, September 30, 1896; XXI, no. 20, May 16, 1905; Rowland Evans, Paul Casey, and Charles Wister, *The Merion Cricket Club, 1865-1965*, Philadelphia, 1965.

34-2 Exterior from east

34-3 Exterior from southwest with porte-cochere

34-4 Porte-cochere, detail

## 35  Franklin Building

**Twelfth and Lawson Streets
Furness, Evans and Co.**

Designed in 1894, concrete foundations were being poured in April 1895, and the building was finished by the fall of the same year. The building's owners, William West Frazier and his brother-in-law Charles Harrison, were among Furness's most valued friends and patrons. Frazier was a member of the building committee of the Seamen's Church, and Furness designed a house for him on Rittenhouse Square, a clubhouse in Jenkintown, and various other structures. Furness designed Harrison's country house, "Happy Creek Farm," and was selected as the designer of the University Library with Harrison's aid. Demolished.

References: *PI:* January 3, 1895, p. 8; March 20, 1895, p. 7; January 26, 1901, p. 11; "Recent Brick and Terra-Cotta Work in American Cities," *Brickbuilder,* IV, November 1895, pp. 242–243; Ellis P. Oberholtzer, *Philadelphia: A History of the City and its People,* Philadelphia, n.d., III, pp. 26–33.

35-1 Exterior from northwest. Courtesy Free Library of Philadelphia

## 36  J. T. Bailey and Company

**Water and Otsego Streets**
**Furness, Evans and Co.**

This long building was built in at least
five stages, each clearly visible on the
façade. The pedimented southernmost
section bears the date 1889. That
immediately to the north supports an
inscription which reads "Burned and
Rebuilt 1882." The central section,
originally four stories high, was designed
by Furness, Evans and Co. in 1895. To
the north of that is another pediment
bearing the date 1885, and to the north
of that the final section, also designed in
1895 by Furness, Evans and Co. The
continuity of detail across the entire length
makes it likely that Furness designed or
remodeled the undocumented sections.

References: *PRERBG*, X, no. 8, February 20,
1895; *PI*, March 27, 1895, p. 5.

36-1 Front Street façade, detail

36-2 Front Street façade, detail of central pavilion with tower removed

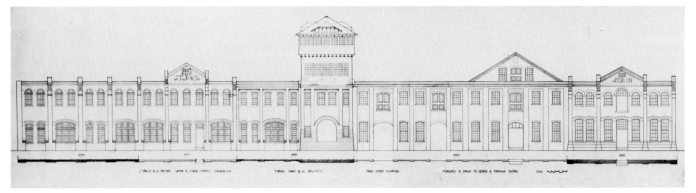
36-3 Front Street elevation reconstructed from old photo-
graphs and existing buildings. Drawn by Marianna Thomas

## 37 Horace Jayne House
## (now Heart Fund Headquarters)

### 320 South Nineteenth Street
### Furness, Evans and Co.

Erected in 1895 for Horace Jayne, M.D., son-in-law of Horace Howard Furness. The building incorporated Dr. Jayne's office. The interior arrangement has been somewhat modified and the original decoration altered.

Reference: *PI,* May 16, 1895, p 5.

37-2 Central hall with balcony above fireplace

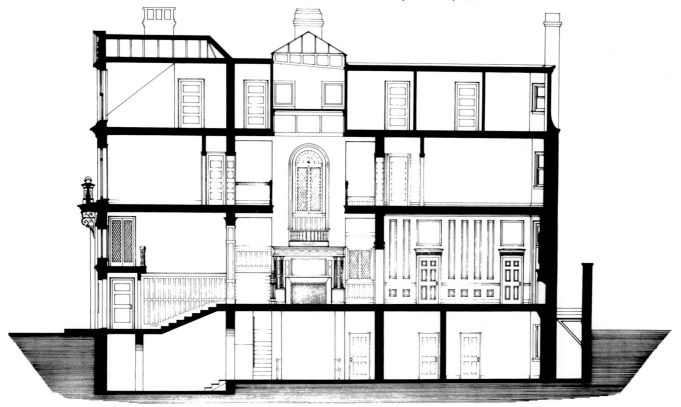

37-3 Longitudinal section. Drawn by Hugh McCauley

37-1 (opposite) Central hall looking toward skylight

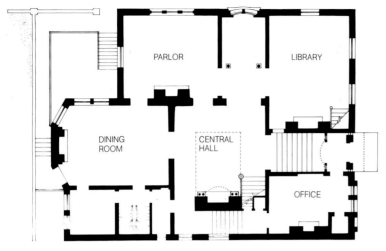

37-4 First-floor plan. Drawn by Hugh McCauley

Within the plan:
PARLOR
LIBRARY
DINING ROOM
CENTRAL HALL
OFFICE

37-5 Window detail, north elevation

37-6 Exterior from east

## 38 Philadelphia Saving Fund Society Building

**Seventh and Walnut Streets**
**Furness, Evans and Co.**

The firm's work of 1897–98 was an addition to Addison Hutton's original building of 1868, which Hutton had extended in 1883–86. George Howe in turn remodeled the bank in 1930.

References: *PI*, June 19, 1897, p. 7; James Wilcox, *A History of the Philadelphia Saving Fund Society 1816–1916*, Philadelphia, 1916, p. 79.

38-1 Main banking room, detail

38-2 Main banking room. Before 1930. Courtesy Philadelphia Saving Fund Society

38-3 Interior looking south. Courtesy Philadelphia Saving Fund Society

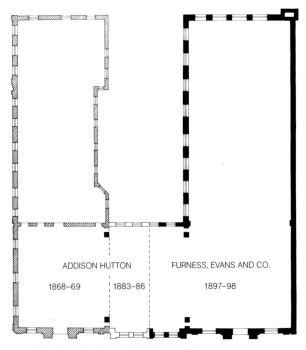

ADDISON HUTTON

1868–69      1883–86

FURNESS, EVANS AND CO.

1897–98

38-4 Phasing plan. Drawn by Marianna Thomas

38-5 Addison Hutton. Philadelphia Saving Fund Society Building from northeast, before additions. Courtesy Philadelphia Saving Fund Society

38-6 Walnut Street façade from northwest

## 39  West End Trust Building

### Broad Street and South Penn Square
### Furness, Evans and Co.

This tall U-shaped office building was erected for a group headed by George B. Roberts, president of the Pennsylvania Railroad. Built in 1898 and enlarged in 1901, it is no longer standing.

References: *PRERBG:* XIII, no. 13, March 30, 1898; XIII, no. 24, June 15, 1898; *PI:* June 9, 1898, p. 13; March 28, 1901, p. 15.

39-1 Exterior from northeast with the Girard Trust to left. Before 1910. Courtesy Historical Society of Pennsylvania, Philadelphia

## 40 Arcade (Commercial Trust) Building

**Fifteenth and Market Streets**
**Furness, Evans and Co.**

In 1894 Joseph Huston of Furness, Evans and Co. proposed the erection of an "arcade building similar to the Galleria Vittorio Emanuele in Milan" on the block between Market and Chestnut at Fifteenth Street. The building (without interior arcade but including the bridge over Market Street) was erected in 1900 for a group of Furness's most important patrons, especially the Pennsylvania Railroad. It was enlarged in 1904 and again after Furness's death. Demolished.

References: *PRERBG,* IX, no. 11, March 14, 1894; *PI:* March 21, 1900, p. 9; January 26, 1901, p. 11; April 5, 1904, p. 9; May 21, 1904, p. 6; Massey 3, p. 11.

40-1 Exterior arcade, detail. Photograph by Jack Boucher. Courtesy *HABS.* Library of Congress, Washington, D.C.

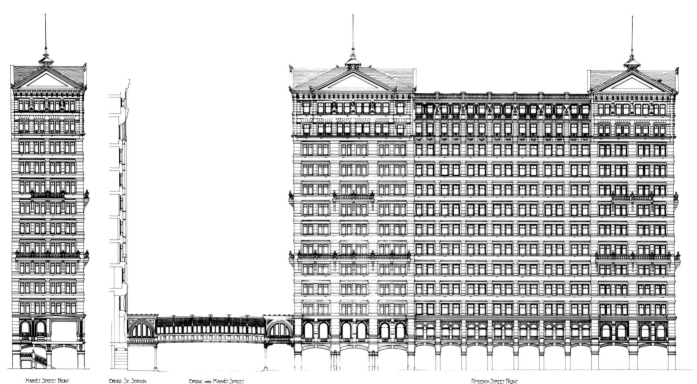

MARKET STREET FRONT    BROAD ST STATION    BRIDGE over MARKET STREET    FIFTEENTH STREET FRONT

40-2 Fifteenth Street and Market Street façades with pedestrian bridge. Redrawn by Marianna Thomas from originals by Furness, Evans and Co.

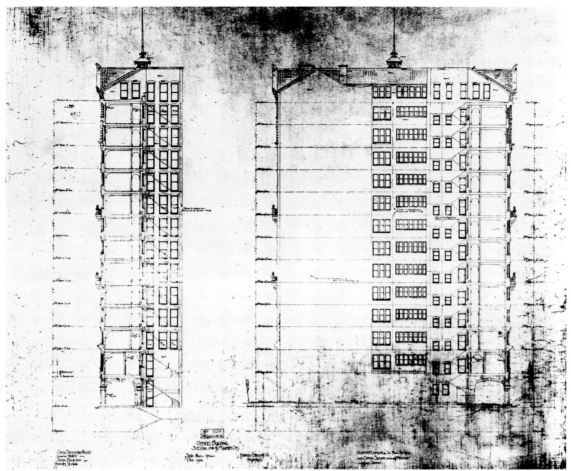

40-3 Furness, Evans and Co. Section through stairhall and arcade. December 1900. Collection Penn-Central Company, Philadelphia

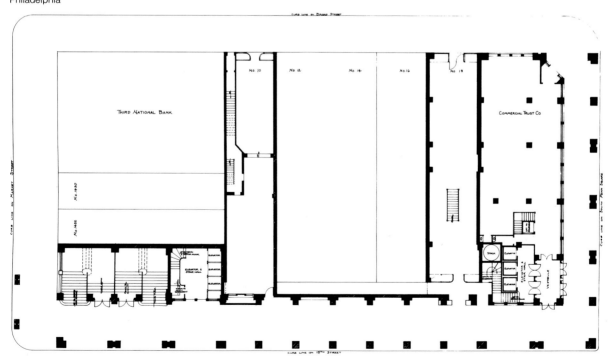

40-4 Plan. Redrawn by Marianna Thomas from original in Collection of Penn-Central Company, Philadelphia

40-5 Exterior, detail. Photograph by Jack Boucher. Courtesy *HABS*. Library of Congress, Washington, D.C.

40-6 Exterior from southeast with later additions

40-7 Broad Street Station with pedestrian bridge over Market Street, from Arcade Building. Courtesy Penn-Central Company, Philadelphia

# Checklist of the Architecture and Projects of Frank Furness

George E. Thomas and Hyman Myers

The checklist is a record of the information known about Furness's commissions at the time of the publication of this volume. The general policy has been to cite the first document only of each commission; thus, there are times when the commission date differs from the construction date given elsewhere in this book. For example, the Williamson Free School was commissioned in 1889 but built between 1890 and 1891. Where no exact date is indicated, the chronology remains uncertain.

All buildings are in Pennsylvania, unless otherwise noted. The addresses cited usually have been taken from the sources and have not been brought up to date.

# Documented Works

## Frank Furness

**1 Germantown Unitarian Church**
Greene Street and Chelten Avenue, Germantown,
Philadelphia
1866–67
Demolished

Records of the congregation; "Minutes of the
Board of Directors for 1866 and 1867 at 6500
Lincoln Drive, Philadelphia" (MS).
(fig. 15)

**2 "Park Cottages"**
Fairmount Park, Philadelphia

"Philadelphia Letter," *AABN*, I, October 14, 1876,
p. 335.

## Fraser, Furness and Hewitt

**3 Alterations to the Franklin Market Company
building for the Mercantile Library Company**
Tenth Street below Market Street, Philadelphia
1867–69
Demolished

*Forty-fifth Annual Report of the Mercantile
Library Company of Philadelphia for 1868*,
Philadelphia, 1868, p. 7.

**4 Competition for the Academy of Natural
Sciences, Philadelphia**
1868
Project
Competition lost to James H. Windrim

Records of the Academy of Natural Sciences.

**5 Church of the Holy Apostles**
Twenty-first and Christian Streets, Philadelphia
1868–70
Altered
Hewitt in charge

William Casner, *The History of the Church of the
Holy Apostles, 1868–1918*, Philadelphia, n.d.,
p. 19.
(cat. 1)

**6 Rodef Shalom Synagogue**
Broad and Mt. Vernon Streets, Philadelphia
1868–69
Demolished

*Proceedings of the Laying of the Corner-Stone
for the Synagogue . . . Rodef Shalom*,
Philadelphia, 1869, *passim*.
(cat. 2)

**7 Alterations to the third-floor meeting rooms
of the Local Chapter of the American Institute
of Architects, The Athenaeum of Philadelphia**
East Washington Square, Philadelphia
1870

"Minutes of the Local Chapter, American
Institute of Architects, Philadelphia Chapter"
(MS), meeting of October 12, 1870.

**8 Lutheran Church of the Holy Communion**
Broad and Arch Streets, Philadelphia
1870–75
Demolished
Later documents mention only Furness and
Hewitt

Signed photo-lithograph in the archives of
successor church, the Evangelical Church of the
Holy Communion, 2100 block, Chestnut Street,
Philadelphia.

**9 St. James Episcopal Church**
Twenty-second and Walnut Streets, Philadelphia
1870–71
Demolished
Hewitt in charge

A. Margaretta Archambault, *A Guide Book of
Art, Architecture and Historical Interests in
Pennsylvania*, Philadelphia, 1924, p. 88.

**10 Extensions to the Armory, First Troop,
Philadelphia City Cavalry**
Twenty-first Street above Chestnut Street,
Philadelphia
1870
Unexecuted

Specifications in the archives, First Troop,
Philadelphia City Cavalry, Twenty-third and
Ranstead Streets, Philadelphia.
(cat. 7)

## Furness and Hewitt

Note: Dissolution of the firm of Fraser, Furness
and Hewitt; replaced by Furness and Hewitt,
September 1, 1871.
Letter to John Sartain from John Fraser,
October 5, 1871, in the archives of the
Pennsylvania Academy of the Fine Arts.

**11 Main building and minor structures, Jewish
Hospital**
Broad Street and Old York Road, Philadelphia
December 1871–September 1873
Demolished

*Ninth Annual Report of the Jewish Hospital
Association of Philadelphia*, Philadelphia, 1874,
pp. 48–51.
(cat. 4)

**12 Pennsylvania Academy of the Fine Arts**
Broad and Cherry Streets, Philadelphia
1871–76

Signed drawings and minutes of the board of
directors in the archives of the Pennsylvania
Academy of the Fine Arts.
(cat. 3)

**13 John Ashhurst residence**
2204 Walnut Street, Philadelphia
Altered

Drawings, filed under Wilson Eyre, in the
Historical Society of Pennsylvania (pointed out
to us by Edward Teitelman).

**14 B. H. Moore residence**
510 South Broad Street, Philadelphia
1872–74
Demolished

Louis Sullivan, *The Autobiography of an Idea*,
New York, 1956, pp. 190–191. Moore's name
appears in Furness's sketchbooks, Collection
George Wood Furness.

**15 Fairman Rogers residence**
Newport, Rhode Island
Altered

C. W. Elliot, *The Book of American Interiors*,
Boston, 1876, Pl. 113.

**16 Philadelphia Warehouse Company**
235 Dock Street, Philadelphia
1872–73
Demolished

*The Philadelphia Sketch-Club*, Philadelphia,
1874, Pl. 10.
(cat. 5)

**17 Alterations to Frank Furness residence**
711 Locust Street, Philadelphia
1873 and later
Demolished

*Artistic Houses*, New York, 1883, II, p. 169.

**18 St. Peter's Episcopal Church, Germantown**
6000 Wayne Avenue, Germantown, Philadelphia
1873
Hewitt in charge

Theodore Rumney and Charles Bullock, *History
of St. Peter's Church, Germantown in the city of
Philadelphia*, Germantown, 1873, p. 6.

**19 Alterations to the Mercantile Library
Company**
Tenth Street below Market Street, Philadelphia
1873
Demolished

Commission recorded in the Furness
sketchbooks, Collection George Wood Furness.

**20 Union Banking Company**
310 Chestnut Street, Philadelphia
1873–74
Demolished

Louis Sullivan, *The Autobiography of an Idea*,
New York, 1956, p. 191. Details of the façade
can be found in the Furness sketchbooks,
Collection George Wood Furness.

**21 St. Timothy's Church and Parish House**
5720 Ridge Avenue, Roxborough, Philadelphia
1873
William M. Camac in charge

*A History of St. Timothy's Church*, Philadelphia,
1949.

**22 Guarantee Trust and Safe Deposit Company**
316–320 Chestnut Street, Philadelphia
1873–75
Demolished

*AABN*, II, September 22, 1877, p. 308.
(cat. 6)

**23 Addition to the Armory, First Troop,
Philadelphia City Cavalry**
Twenty-first and Barker Streets, Philadelphia
1874
Demolished

*AABN*, I, October 14, 1876, p. 335.
(cat. 7)

**24 Alterations to Fred Brown residence**
2036 Delancey Street, Philadelphia

Commission recorded in the Furness
sketchbooks, Collection George Wood Furness.

**25 Church of the Holy Comforter**
Nineteenth and Titan Streets, Philadelphia
1874

"T Street Church" in the Furness sketchbooks,
Collection George Wood Furness.

**26 Alterations to Rudolph Ellis residence**
2113 Spruce Street, Philadelphia

*Artistic Houses*, New York, 1883, I, pp. 165ff.

**27 Rowland Evans residence: "Penrhyn-y-Coed"**
Haverford
1874
Demolished

Documents in collection of Allen Evans III, Bryn Mawr.

**28 Alterations to Children's Hospital**
207 South Twenty-second Street, Philadelphia
Demolished

Commission recorded in the Furness sketchbooks, Collection George Wood Furness.

**29 Charles Cushman residence: "Brynhild"**
Lancaster Pike, Radnor
1874
Demolished

S. F. Hotchkin, *Rural Pennsylvania*, Philadelphia, 1897, p. 182.

**30 Addition to the Pennsylvania Institution for the Deaf and Dumb**
Broad and Pine Streets, Philadelphia
1874–75

*The Annual Report of the Board of Directors of the Pennsylvania Institution for the Deaf and Dumb for the Year 1875*, Philadelphia, 1876, p. 7.
(cat. 8)

**31 H. W. Catherwood residence**
1708 Walnut Street, Philadelphia
1874
Altered

Commission recorded in the Furness sketchbooks, Collection George Wood Furness.

**32 Alterations to Horace Howard Furness residence**
222 West Washington Square, Philadelphia
Demolished

Massey 2, p. 26.

**33 St. Luke's Parish House**
330 South Thirteenth Street, Philadelphia

Commission recorded in the Furness sketchbooks, Collection George Wood Furness.

**34 Thomas Hockley residence**
235 South Twenty-first Street, Philadelphia
1875
Altered

*Philadelphia Press*, July 5, 1885, p. 12.
(cat. 9)

**35 Alterations and additions to the Women's Medical College**
North College Avenue, Philadelphia
Demolished

Commission recorded in the Furness sketchbooks, Collection George Wood Furness.

**36 Gatehouse, Philadelphia Zoological Gardens**
Thirty-fourth Street and Girard Avenue, Philadelphia
1875–76

*Fourth Annual Report of the Board of Managers of the Zoological Society of Philadelphia*, Philadelphia, 1876, p. 9.
(cat. 11)

**37 Restaurant, Philadelphia Zoological Gardens**
Thirty-fourth Street and Girard Avenue, Philadelphia
1875–76
Demolished

Records of the Philadelphia Zoological Society; drawings in the Furness sketchbooks, Collection George Wood Furness. (Rebuilt by George Hewitt in 1898. *PI*, December 5, 1899, p. 9.)
(cat. 11)

**38 Elephant House, Philadelphia Zoological Gardens**
Thirty-fourth Street and Girard Avenue, Philadelphia
1875–76
Demolished

*Third Annual Report of the Board of Managers of the Zoological Society of Philadelphia*, Philadelphia, 1875, p. 11.
(cat. 11)

**39 Jefferson Medical College Hospital**
Tenth and Sansom Streets, Philadelphia
1875–77
Demolished

Records of Thomas Jefferson University; *AABN*, I, September 9, 1876, p. 292.
(cat. 10)

**40 West Philadelphia Hall**
3316 Market Street, Philadelphia
1875–76
Demolished

Commission recorded in the Furness sketchbooks, Collection George Wood Furness.

# Frank Furness

**41 Institute for Feeble Minded Children**
Lincoln, Illinois
1875–77
Demolished
Frank Furness, Laing and Fehmer, Architects

*AABN*, II, February 10, 1877, p. 44; recorded in the Furness sketchbooks, Collection George Wood Furness.

**42 Brazilian Pavilion**
Main Building, Centennial Exhibition, Philadelphia
1876
Demolished

*AABN*, I, May 13, 1876, p. 160.
(cat. 12)

**43 Roxborough Baptist Church**
5705 Ridge Avenue, Roxborough, Philadelphia
1876

Drawings, Collection George Wood Furness.

**44 Centennial National Bank**
Thirty-second and Market Streets, Philadelphia
1876
Altered

*AABN*, I, December 23, 1876, p. 414.
(cat. 13)

**45 The Provident Life and Trust Company**
409 Chestnut and 42 South Fourth Streets, Philadelphia
1876–79
Demolished
Other competitors included George Hewitt, James H. Windrim, and Addison Hutton

"Minutes of the Board of Directors of the Provident Life and Trust Company" (MS), meeting of August 7, 1876.
(cat. 14)

**46 Shamokin Station, Philadelphia and Reading Railroad**
Shamokin
1876
Perhaps unexecuted

Signed, dated drawing in collection of Mr. and Mrs. Alfred W. Hesse, Jr., Gladwyne.
(fig. 34)

**47 The Honorable J. Clarke Hare residence**
118 South Twenty-second Street, Philadelphia
Demolished

Commission recorded in the Furness sketchbooks, Collection George Wood Furness.

**48 Kensington National Bank**
Frankford and Girard Avenues, Philadelphia
Completed August 1877
Altered

*AABN*, II, August 25, 1877, p. 273.
(cat. 15)

**49 Hotel entrance**
Chestnut Street, Philadelphia
1876
Demolished

*AABN*, I, October 14, 1876, pp. 334–336.

**50 Three-story building for Jefferson Medical College**
130 South Tenth Street, Philadelphia
1877
Demolished

*AABN*, II, August 25, 1877, p. 273.
(cat. 10)

**51 Renovations to the Mercantile Library Company after fire damage**
Tenth Street below Market Street, Philadelphia
1877
Demolished

*AABN*, II, August 25, 1877, p. 273.

**52 Lunatic Asylum, Philadelphia**
Project
Competition lost; competitors included Hutton and Ord, Collins and Autenrieth, Samuel Sloan, and others

*AABN*, II, September 22, 1877, p. 306.

**53 Stenciled decorations for St. Stephen's Church**
Tenth Street below Market Street, Philadelphia
July 1878
Altered

"Minutes of St. Stephen's Church" (MS), meeting of July 3, 1878.

**54 Church of the Redeemer for Seamen and Their Families and Charles Brewer School**
Front and Queen Streets, Philadelphia
1878

"Records of the Board of Managers, Churchmen's Missionary Association for Seamen of the Port of Philadelphia" (MS), meeting of September 10, 1878; records in possession of the Seamen's Church Institute, 1212 Locust Street, Philadelphia.
(cat. 16)

**55 Loeb Dispensary, Jewish Hospital**
Broad Street and Old York Road, Philadelphia
1878
Demolished

Records of the Einstein Medical Center, Philadelphia.
(cat. 4)

**56 Allen Evans residence**
Lower Merion
1878
Demolished

Records in collection of Allen Evans III, Bryn Mawr.

**57 Additions and alterations to St. Stephen's Church**
Tenth Street below Market Street, Philadelphia
1878-79

"Minutes of St. Stephen's Church" (MS), meeting of October 7, 1878.

**58 Library Company of Philadelphia**
Locust and Juniper Streets, Philadelphia
1879-80
Demolished

*Public Ledger*, February 20, 1879, p. 3.
(cat. 17)

**59 Stable and coachman's dwelling for A. J. Cassatt**
2006 Sansom Street, Philadelphia
1880

*AABN*, VII, February 28, 1880, p. 88.

**60 William H. Rhawn residence: "Knowlton"**
8001 Verree Road, Fox Chase, Philadelphia
1880

*AABN*, VII, February 28, 1880, p. 88.
(cat. 18)

**61 The Honorable John Welsh residence**
Chestnut Hill, Philadelphia
1880
Demolished

*AABN*, VII, February 28, 1880, p. 88.

**62 J. R. Williams residence**
Haverford
1880
Allen Evans in charge

*AABN*, VII, February 28, 1880, p. 88.

**63 Stone and timber house for John Lowber Welsh**
Chestnut Hill, Philadelphia
1880

*AABN*, VII, February 28, 1880, p. 88.

**64 E. C. Evans, M.D., residence**
Haverford
1880
Demolished
Allen Evans in charge

*AABN*, VII, February 28, 1880, p. 88.

**65 The Honorable J. Clarke Hare residence**
Radnor
1880
Allen Evans in charge

*AABN*, VII, March 6, 1880, p. 100.

**66 Additions to Samuel Shipley residence**
1034 Spruce Street, Philadelphia
Demolished

Conversations with Mrs. Page Allinson, daughter of Samuel Shipley, July 1972.

**67 M. R. Thomas residence**
West Chester
1880

*AABN*, VII, March 6, 1880, p. 100.

**68 Alterations to the offices of the Philadelphia and Reading Railroad Company**
Fourth Street and Willings Alley, Philadelphia
1880
Demolished

*AABN*, VII, May 29, 1880, p. 242.

**69 Graver's Lane Station, Philadelphia and Reading Railroad**
Chestnut Hill, Philadelphia

Signed drawings in the archives of the Philadelphia and Reading Railroad Company, Philadelphia.
(cat. 19)

**70 Tabor Station, Philadelphia and Reading Railroad**
Philadelphia
Demolished

Walter Berg, *Buildings and Structures of American Railroads*, New York, 1892, pp. 268-269.

## Furness and Evans

**71 William Peddle Henszey residence: "Red Leaf"**
Lancaster Avenue, Wynnewood
1881
All but carriage house demolished

S. F. Hotchkin, *Rural Pennsylvania*, Philadelphia, 1897, p. 121.

**72 Rowland Evans residence**
Haverford
1881

S. F. Hotchkin, *Rural Pennsylvania*, Philadelphia, 1897, p. 121.

**73 William West Frazier residence**
250 South Eighteenth Street, Philadelphia
1881-82
Demolished

*AABN*, IX, April 30, 1881, p. 216.

**74 Commercial Union Assurance Company**
330 Walnut Street, Philadelphia
1881
Demolished

*Carpenter and Building*, III, October 1881, p. 182.

**75 Additions and alterations to the American Fire Insurance Company**
308-310 Walnut Street, Philadelphia
1881

*Carpenter and Building*, III, October 1881, p. 182.

**76 Clement Griscom residence: "Dolobran"**
Haverford
1881
Altered

Furness was Griscom's architect for all of his major projects, and had a close and continuous professional relationship with "Dolobran." Cf. *PRERBG*, IX, no. 35, August 29, 1894.
(cat. 20)

**77 Reliance Insurance Company**
429 Walnut Street, Philadelphia
1881-82
Demolished

Massey 2, p. 25.

**78 Samuel Shipley residence: "Winden"**
West Chester
1882

Massey 2, p. 26; conversations with Samuel Shipley's daughter, Mrs. Page Allinson, July 1972.
(cat. 22)

**79 Penn National Bank**
Seventh and Market Streets, Philadelphia
1882-84
Demolished

Tremaine's Architectural Photographers lists Furness and Evans as the architects. Photograph in the Penrose Collection, Historical Society of Pennsylvania.
(cat. 21)

**80 Undine Barge Club**
East River Drive, Philadelphia
1882-83

Louis Heiland, *The Undine Barge Club of Philadelphia*, Philadelphia, 1925.
(cat. 23)

**81 National Bank of the Republic**
313 Chestnut Street, Philadelphia
1883-84
Demolished

*AABN*, XV, January 26, 1884, p. 48.
(cat. 25)

**82 First Unitarian Church and Parish House**
Chestnut and Van Pelt Streets, Philadelphia
1883-86
Altered

*PRERBG*, I, no. 6, February 15, 1886.
(cat. 24)

**83 Designs for the remodeling of the ferryboat *Communipaw* for the Philadelphia and Reading Railroad Company**

Letter from Frank Furness to John E. Wooten, December 23, 1884, in the Historical Society of Pennsylvania (this document was uncovered by John Stock).

**84 New work and alterations to existing buildings, totaling 125 structures for the Philadelphia and Reading Railroad Company**
1879-84
Most demolished

Letter from Frank Furness to John E. Wooten, December 23, 1884, in the Historical Society of Pennsylvania.

**85 Seven designs for passenger and parlor cars for the Philadelphia and Reading Railroad Company**

Letter from Frank Furness to John E. Wooten, December 23, 1884, in the Historical Society of Pennsylvania.

**86 George B. Preston residence**
2135 Walnut Street, Philadelphia
1884–85
Demolished

*Philadelphia Press*, July 5, 1885, p. 12.

**87 Farmer's Deposit National Bank**
66 (later 220) Fourth Avenue, Pittsburgh
Demolished

Maximillian Nirdlinger, "Memoirs," MS in the possession of James Van Trump, Pittsburgh, Pa. Nirdlinger was in Furness's office between 1897 and 1899.

**88 Thomas McKean residence**
Germantown, Philadelphia

Drawing, Collection George Wood Furness.

**89 Henry McCall residence**
Germantown, Philadelphia
Demolished

Drawing, Collection George Wood Furness.

**90 Home for Consumptives for the Philadelphia Protestant Episcopal City Mission**
Stenton Avenue at Evergreen Avenue, Chestnut Hill, Philadelphia
1885
Altered

S. F. Hotchkin, *Ancient and Modern Germantown, Mount Airy and Chestnut Hill*, Philadelphia 1889, p. 440.

## Furness, Evans and Company

Note: Furness and Evans become Furness, Evans and Company in 1886 when Louis C. Baker, E. James Dallett, William M. Camac, and James W. Fassitt were made partners in the firm. *Illustrated Philadelphia, Its Wealth and Industries*, New York, 1889, p. 174.

**91 Hotel at Lake Hopatcong**
Morris County, New Jersey
1886
Demolished
L. C. Baker in charge

*PRERBG*, I, no. 6, February 15, 1886.

**92 Actress Latta's residence**
Lake Hopatcong
Morris County, New Jersey
1886
L. C. Baker in charge

*PRERBG*, I, no. 18, May 10, 1886.

**93 Bailey, Banks and Biddle factory**
Twelfth and Sansom Streets, Philadelphia
1886
Demolished

*PRERBG*, I, no. 20, May 24, 1886.

**94 Church of the Evangelists**
Seventh and Catharine Streets, Philadelphia
1886
Altered
L. C. Baker in charge

*PRERBG*, I, no. 21, May 31, 1886.

**95 Four houses**
Hart Lane at Frankford Road, Philadelphia
1886

*PRERBG*, I, no. 21, May 31, 1886.

**96 J. G. Blaine residence**
Mount Desert Island, Bar Harbor, Maine
1886

*PRERBG*, I, no. 21, May 31, 1886.

**97 Alterations and additions to the American Fire Insurance Company Building**
308–310 Walnut Street, Philadelphia
1886

*PRERBG*, I, no. 25, June 28, 1886.

**98 Philadelphia Station, Baltimore and Ohio Railroad**
Twenty-fourth and Chestnut Streets, Philadelphia
1886–88
Demolished

*PRERBG*, I, no. 32, August 16, 1886.
(cat. 26)

**99 Chester Station, Baltimore and Ohio Railroad**
Chester
1886
Demolished

Drawings in the Historical Society of Pennsylvania.
(cat. 27)

**100 Belaire Station, Baltimore and Ohio Railroad**
Delaware and DuPont Streets, Wilmington, Delaware
1886
Demolished

Drawings in the manuscript department of the Historical Society of Pennsylvania.

**101 Gorgas Home for Indigent Women**
East Leverington Avenue, Roxborough, Philadelphia
1886–87

*PRERBG*, I, no. 37, September 20, 1886.

**102 I. Layton Register residence: "Lynnhurst"**
Ardmore

S. F. Hotchkin, *Rural Pennsylvania*, Philadelphia, 1897, p. 118.

**103 Hotel**
Eager and Charles Streets, Baltimore, Maryland
1887–88
Demolished

*PRERBG*, II, no. 41, October 17, 1887.

**104 Forty-six houses**
Diamond Street between Sixteenth and Seventeenth Streets, Philadelphia

*PRERBG*, II, no. 15, April 18, 1887.

**105 William Winsor residence: "Hedgely"**
Ardmore
1887–88
Altered

Signed drawings, Collection Winsor family, Ardmore.
(cat. 28)

**106 Dr. Henry C. Register residence: "Mill Creek"**
Lower Merion

S. F. Hotchkin, *Rural Pennsylvania*, Philadelphia, 1897, p. 118.

**107 Livingston House**
2202 Walnut Street, Philadelphia
1887
Demolished

*PRERBG*, II, no. 41, October 17, 1887.

**108 Villas for the Department for the Insane of the Pennsylvania Hospital**
Forty-eighth and Market Streets, Philadelphia
1887–88
Demolished

*Annual Report of the Department for the Insane of the Pennsylvania Hospital*, Philadelphia, 1888, p. 15.

**109 Sketch for building at Broad and Chestnut Streets**
Philadelphia
1888

*Fifty-eighth Annual Exhibition of the Pennsylvania Academy of the Fine Arts*, Philadelphia, 1888, no. 539.

**110 Frenchtown Station, Baltimore and Ohio Railroad**
Frenchtown, Maryland
1888
Demolished

Drawings in the manuscript department of the Historical Society of Pennsylvania.

**111 Wilmington Station, Baltimore and Ohio Railroad**
Front and Market Streets, Wilmington, Delaware
1888
Demolished

Drawings in the Historical Society of Pennsylvania.

**112 Additions and alterations to the Philadelphia Club**
Thirteenth and Walnut Streets, Philadelphia
1888

*Builder, Decorator and Woodworker*, VII, no. 3, November 1888.

**113 William Patton residence: "Crestlinn"**
Radnor
1888

S. F. Hotchkin, *Rural Pennsylvania*, Philadelphia, 1897, p. 222.

**114 Baltimore and Ohio Railroad Terminal**
Pittsburgh
1888
Demolished

James Van Trump, "Pittsburgh Railroad Station," *Charette*, XXVIII, January 1956, pp. 21–30.

**115 Home for the Aged and Infirm Israelites, Jewish Hospital**
Broad Street and Old York Road, Philadelphia
1888
Demolished

*PRERBG*, III, no. 2, January 16, 1888.
(cat. 4)

**116 Boiler house, Jewish Hospital**
Broad Street and Old York Road, Philadelphia
1888
Demolished

*Twenty-fourth Annual Report of the Jewish Hospital Association*, Philadelphia, 1889, p. 68.
(cat. 4)

**117 Laundry building, Jewish Hospital**
Broad Street and Old York Road, Philadelphia
1888
Demolished

*Twenty-fourth Annual Report of the Jewish
Hospital Association*, Philadelphia, 1889, p. 68.
(cat. 4)

**118 Kitchen building, Jewish Hospital**
Broad Street and Old York Road, Philadelphia
1888
Demolished

*Twenty-fourth Annual Report of the Jewish
Hospital Association*, Philadelphia, 1889, p. 68.
(cat. 4)

**119 The Provident Life and Trust Company**
401 Chestnut Street, Philadelphia
1888–90
Demolished
Other competitors included George C. Mason
(Newport, R.I.), William Emerson (Boston), and
George T. Pearson (Philadelphia)

"Minutes of the Board of Directors of the
Provident Life and Trust Company" (MS),
meeting of February 13, 1888.
(cat. 14)

**120 Library Building, University of Pennsylvania**
Thirty-fourth Street and Woodland Avenue,
Philadelphia
1888–91
Altered

*PRERBG*, III, no. 28, July 16, 1888.
(cat. 29)

**121 Cottage for Frank Furness: "Idlewild"**
Media

Conversations with George Wood Furness.
(fig. 38)

**122 George Fox residence**
Old York Road, Ashbourne
Demolished

S. F. Hotchkin, *Old York Road*, Philadelphia,
1892, p. 153.

**123 Caleb Fox residence**
Old York Road, Ashbourne
Demolished

S. F. Hotchkin, *Old York Road*, Philadelphia,
1892, p. 153.

**124 Frederick Fox residence**
Old York Road, Ashbourne
Demolished

S. F. Hotchkin, *Old York Road*, Philadelphia,
1892, p. 153.

**125 Frank Thompson residence:
"Corkerhill"**
Union Avenue, Lower Merion
1889
Demolished

*PRERBG*, IV, no. 6, February 13, 1889.

**126 St. Michael's and All the Angels Church**
Forty-second and Wallace Streets, Philadelphia
1889
Altered or unexecuted
William M. Camac in charge

*PRERBG*, IV, no. 23, June 12, 1889.

**127 Alterations to the Racquet Club**
923 Walnut Street, Philadelphia
1889
Demolished

*PRERBG*, IV, no. 30, July 21, 1889.

**128 Williamson Free School of Mechanical
Trades**
Middletown Road, Elwyn
1889–90
Altered
Other competitors included Wilson Brothers,
G. W. and W. D. Hewitt, Thomas P. Lonsdale,
Cope and Stewardson

*PI*, August 24, 1889, p. 3.
(cat. 30)

**129 Alterations to 2109 Spruce Street**
Philadelphia
1889

*PRERBG*, IV, no. 34, August 28, 1889.

**130 Bryn Mawr Hotel for the Bryn Mawr Hotel
Company of the Pennsylvania Railroad**
Bryn Mawr
1890

*PI*, January 26, 1890, p. 7.
(cat. 31)

**131 Additions to George Gerhard residence**
Ardmore
1890
Demolished

*PI*, June 3, 1890, p. 7.

**132 Alterations and additions to 1221–1223
Locust Street**
Philadelphia
1890
Altered

*Builder, Decorator and Woodworker*, XIV, no. 5,
July 1890.

**133 Alterations and additions to houses at
Twelfth and Locust Streets**
Philadelphia
1890
Altered and/or demolished

*Builder, Decorator and Woodworker*, XIV, no. 5,
July 1890.

**134 Alterations to John G. Blaine residence**
2000 Massachusetts Avenue, N.W.,
Washington, D.C.
1890–91
Altered

*PI*, August 27, 1890, p. 7.

**135 Additions to Thomas DeWitt Cuyler
residence**
Haverford
1890
Demolished

*PI*, October 7, 1890, p. 7.

**136 Alumni Memorial Hall, University of
Pennsylvania**
Thirty-fourth and Spruce Streets, Philadelphia
1890
Unexecuted

*PI*, October 27, 1890, p. 6.

**137 Charles C. Harrison residence:
"Happy Creek Farm"**
Devon

S. F. Hotchkin, *Rural Pennsylvania*,
Philadelphia, 1897, p. 289.

**138 1804 Rittenhouse Square**
Philadelphia
1891–92
George W. Casey in charge

*Sixty-second Annual Exhibition, Pennsylvania
Academy of the Fine Arts*, Philadelphia, 1892,
no. 488.

**139 Percy C. Madeira residence**
Ogontz, Philadelphia
1891
Demolished

*PI*, January 14, 1891, p. 7.

**140 Reconstruction of 1820 Delancey Street**
Philadelphia
1891

*PI*, March 11, 1891, p. 7.

**141 Additional structures for the Home for
Consumptives for the Philadelphia Protestant
Episcopal City Mission**
Stenton Avenue at Evergreen Avenue,
Chestnut Hill, Philadelphia
1891–92

*PI*, March 12, 1891, p. 7.

**142 Alterations to 1821 Delancey Street**
Philadelphia
1891

*PRERBG*, VI, no. 11, March 18, 1891.

**143 New wing, Pennsylvania Hospital for
the Insane**
Forty-eighth and Market Streets, Philadelphia
1891

*PI*, April 22, 1891, p. 7.

**144 Department for Females, Pennsylvania
Hospital for the Insane**
Forty-eighth and Market Streets, Philadelphia
1891
Demolished

*PRERBG*, VI, no. 17, April 29, 1891.

**145 Episcopal Chapel**
Eleventh and Snyder Streets,
Philadelphia
1891
Demolished

*Builder, Decorator and Woodworker*,
XVI, no. 4, June 1891.

**146 Recitation Hall,
Delaware State College**
Newark, Delaware
1891
Altered

*PI*, July 8, 1891, p. 7.

**147 Oratory building,
Delaware State College**
Newark, Delaware
1891
Altered

*PRERBG*, VI, no. 28, July 15, 1891.

**148 Clubhouse**
Lansdowne
1891

*PI*, July 21, 1891, p. 7.

**149 H. Allen residence**
1524 North Seventh Street,
Philadelphia
1891

*PRERBG*, VI, no. 30, July 27, 1891.

**150 New stable for Frank Thompson estate**
Merion
1891
Demolished

*PI*, October 1, 1891, p. 7.

**151 Mortuary Chapel, Mount Sinai Cemetery**
Bridge and Cottage Streets, Frankford,
Philadelphia
1891–92

*PI*, February 27, 1892, p. 7.
(cat. 32)

**152 First National Bank of Darby**
Darby
1892
George W. Casey in charge

*Sixty-second Annual Exhibition of the
Pennsylvania Academy of the Fine Arts,*
Philadelphia, 1892, no. 489.

**153 Merion Cricket Club**
Montgomery Avenue, Haverford
1892
Demolished

Rowland Evans, Paul Casey and Charles
Wister, *The Merion Cricket Club, 1865–1965,*
Philadelphia, 1965.
(cat. 34)

**154 Church of Our Saviour**
Jenkintown
1892

*PRERBG*, XII, no. 2, January 13, 1892.

**155 Additions to the Provident Life and
Trust Company**
Fourth and Chestnut Streets, Philadelphia
1892
Demolished

*PI*, February 11, 1892, p. 7.
(cat. 14)

**156 Rebuilding of 627 Market Street**
Philadelphia
1892
Demolished

*PRERBG*, VII, no. 10, March 9, 1892.

**157 Additions and alterations to Christ
Church Chapel**
1915–1923 Pine Street, Philadelphia
Altered

*PI*, May 21, 1892, p. 7.

**158 Chapel and Parish House, Church of the
Atonement**
Forty-seventh Street and Kingsessing Avenue,
Philadelphia
1892

*PI*, June 30, 1892, p. 7.

**159 Bryn Mawr Hospital**
Bryn Mawr
1892

*PI*, July 19, 1892, p. 7.

**160 Additions to the Broad Street Station,
Pennsylvania Railroad**
Broad and Market Streets, Philadelphia
1892–93
Demolished

*PRERBG*, VII, no. 30, July 27, 1892.
(cat. 33)

**161 Reconstruction of 1222–1224 Locust Street**
Philadelphia
1892
Demolished

*PI*, October 14, 1892, p. 8.

**162 Alterations to a building for the Lucien
Moss estate**
267 South Twenty-first Street, Philadelphia
1892

*PRERBG*, VII, no. 44, November 2, 1892.

**163 Open letter requesting that the Harrisburg
public buildings be an open competition**
Signed by Frank Furness, Samuel Huckle,
A. J. Boyden, James H. Windrim, T. P. Chandler,
George C. Mason, Allen Evans, Wilson Eyre,
F. M. Day, Jos. Wilson, February 8, 1893.

**164 Parish House, Church of Our Saviour**
Jenkintown
1893
Altered

*PRERBG*, VIII, no. 15, April 12, 1893.

**165 Boiler house stack, Girard College**
Philadelphia
1893

*PRERBG*, VIII, no. 34, August 23, 1893.

**166 Thomas Riley stable**
Maloney Street west of Twentieth Street,
Philadelphia
1894

*PRERBG*, IX, no. 4, January 24, 1894.

**167 Colonial style residence**
Main and Carpenter Streets,
Germantown, Philadelphia
1894

*PRERBG*, IX, no. 6, February 7, 1894.

**168 Alterations to the original segment of the
Broad Street Station, Pennsylvania Railroad**
Broad and Filbert Streets, Philadelphia
1894
Demolished

*PRERBG*, IX, no. 8, February 21, 1894.
(cat. 33)

**169 Addition to the Nixon residence**
842 North Broad Street, Philadelphia
1894
Demolished

*PI*, March 8, 1894, p. 12.

**170 Alterations to 2210 Walnut Street, made
necessary by the change in level caused by the
building of the Walnut Street Bridge**
Philadelphia
1894
Demolished

*PRERBG*, IX, no. 17, April 25, 1894.

**171 Good Samaritan Hospital**
Broad and Ontario Streets, Philadelphia
1894
Joseph Huston in charge

*PRERBG*, IX, no. 23, June 6, 1894.

**172 Barclay Warburton stable**
2058 Sansom Street, Philadelphia
1894
Altered

*PI*, June 27, 1894, p. 9.

**173 Alterations to 1023 Market Street**
Philadelphia
1894
Altered

*PRERBG*, IX, no. 35, August 29, 1894.

**174 Temporary building of great size built of
staff, for Frank Thompson**
Merion
1894
Demolished

*PRERBG*, IX, no. 35, August 29, 1894.

**175 "Old Parsonage" retirement home**
Baltimore, Maryland
1894

*Inland Architect*, XXIII, no. 5, June 1894.

**176 Alterations to Clement Griscom residence:
"Dolobran"**
Haverford
1894

*PRERBG*, IX, no. 35, August 29, 1894.
(cat. 20)

**177 G. W. Childs residence**
K Street near Sixteenth Street, N. W.,
Washington, D.C.
1894
Demolished

*PRERBG*, IX, no. 42, October 17, 1894.

**178 Six-story building for Armstrong Wilkens
and Company**
Fourth Street and Appletree Alley,
Philadelphia
1894
Demolished

*PRERBG*, IX, no. 49, December 5, 1894.

**179 Design of the interiors of two steamships,
the *St. Paul* and the *St. Louis*, for Clement
Griscom**
The American Line
1894–95

*Scientific American*, LXXII, no. 24, June 15,
1895, p. 376.
(see cat. 20)

**180 Franklin Building**
Twelfth and Lawson Streets,
Philadelphia
1894–95
Demolished

*PI*, January 3, 1895, p. 8.
(cat. 35)

**181 Additional wings, Pennsylvania Hospital**
Eighth and Pine Streets,
Philadelphia
Probably unexecuted

Original drawing, Collection of the Pennsylvania
Hospital, Philadelphia.

**182 Addition to John T. Bailey and Company
factory**
Water and Otsego Streets, Philadelphia
1895
Altered

*PRERBG*, X, no. 8, February 20, 1895.
(cat. 36)

**183 Alterations to 34 South Third Street**
Philadelphia
1895
Demolished

*PRERBG*, X, no. 10, March 6, 1895.

**184 Additions to Meyer Sultzberger residence**
1305 Girard Avenue, Philadelphia
1895
Demolished

*PRERBG*, X, no. 16, April 17, 1895.

**185 Horace Jayne residence**
320 South Nineteenth Street,
Philadelphia
1895

*PI*, May 16, 1895, p. 5.
(cat. 37)

**186 Offices of M. J. Earl**
925 Penn Street, Reading

Illustrated handbill in collection of Allen Evans
III, Bryn Mawr.

**187 Five-story building for the New York
Biscuit Company**
Evelina Street east of Third Street,
Philadelphia
1895
Demolished

*PI*, November 2, 1895, p. 8.

**188 Rebuilding of Merion Cricket Club after
fire**
Montgomery Avenue, Haverford
1895
Partially demolished

*PI*, November 2, 1895, p. 8.
(cat. 34)

**189 Additions and Alterations to Thomas
DeWitt Cuyler residence**
1830 Delancey Street, Philadelphia
1896

*PRERBG*, XI, no. 4, January 22, 1896.

**190 Public Baths**
Gaskill and Berlin Streets,
Philadelphia
1896
Altered

*PI*, January 24, 1896, p.10.

**191 Store and warehouse for J. Withens**
Fourth Street and Appletree Alley,
Philadelphia
1896
Demolished

*PI*, February 26, 1896, p. 9.

**192 Alterations to the Holy Trinity Mission**
Twentieth (probably Twenty-second) and
Morris Streets, Philadelphia
1896
Demolished

*PRERBG*, XI, no. 31, July 29, 1896.

**193 Alterations to Miss M. J. Hay residence**
1823 Delancey Street, Philadelphia
1896

*PRERBG*, XI, no. 31, July 29, 1896.

**194 Rosemont Hospital of the Good Shepherd**
Rosemont
1896

*PI*, July 3, 1896, p. 7.

**195 Rebuilding of Merion Cricket Club after
second fire**
Montgomery Avenue, Haverford
1896-97

*PRERBG*, XI, no. 40, September 30, 1896.
(cat. 34)

**196 Additions and alterations to the Hotel
Windsor**
Illinois Avenue and the Boardwalk,
Atlantic City, New Jersey
1896-97
Demolished

*PRERBG*, XI, no. 52, December 23, 1896.

**197 Additions to 400 Arch Street**
Philadelphia
1896-97
Demolished

*PI*, December 30, 1896, p. 11.

**198 Baker Building**
Lansdowne
1896
Morgan Bunting in charge

S. F. Hotchkin, *Rural Pennsylvania*, Philadelphia,
1897, pp. 408-410.

**199 Additions to the Church of Our Saviour**
Jenkintown
1897

*PI*, January 15, 1897, p. 11.

**200 G. R. Griscom residence**
Haverford
1897

*PRERBG*, XII, no. 3, January 20, 1897.

**201 R. E. Griscom residence**
Haverford
1897

*PRERBG*, XII, no. 4, January 27, 1897.

**202 Lucien Moss Home for Incurables, Jewish
Hospital**
Broad Street and Old York Road, Philadelphia
1897
Demolished

*PI*, March 5, 1897, p. 13.
(cat. 4)

**203 St. Nathanael's Parish House**
Allegheny Avenue and E Street,
Philadelphia
1897

*PI*, July 17, 1897, p. 11.

**204 Designs for the Harrisburg State
Capitol building**
1897
Competition lost

*PRERBG*, no. 37, September 15, 1897.

**205 Open letter to the Philadelphia Chapter
of the American Institute of Architects**
Philadelphia, September 25, 1897.

**206 F. L. DuBasque residence**
South Orange, New Jersey
1897

*PRERBG*, XII, no. 39, September 29, 1897.

**207 Pennsylvania Railroad Station**
Morrisville
1897
Demolished

*PI*, November 27, 1897, p. 10.

**208 Additions and alterations to Philadelphia
Saving Fund Society**
Seventh and Walnut Streets,
Philadelphia
1897-98
Altered

James Wilcox, *A History of the Philadelphia
Saving Fund Society 1816-1916*, Philadelphia,
1916, p. 79.
(cat. 38)

**209 Rebuilding of Allen Evans residence**
Haverford

*PI*, January 21, 1898, p. 14.

**210 J. B. Cassatt stable**
Berwyn
1898

*PRERBG*, XIII, no. 11, March 16, 1898.

**211 West End Trust Company Building**
Broad Street and South Penn Square,
Philadelphia
1898
Demolished

*PRERBG*, XIII, no. 13, March 30, 1898.
(cat. 39)

**212 Axel Peterson residence**
Johnson Street and Germantown Avenue,
Philadelphia
1898

*PI*, July 15, 1898, p. 10.

**213 Consumptives Ward and Sun Parlor,
Jewish Hospital**
Broad Street and Old York Road,
Philadelphia
1899
Demolished

*PI*, May 4, 1899, p. 9.
(cat. 4)

**214 Stable at "Chesterbrook Farms"**
Berwyn
1898

*PRERBG*, XIII, no. 29, July 20, 1898.

**215 Harrison Day Nursery**
Nineteenth and Ellsworth Streets,
Philadelphia
1899

*PI*, April 20, 1899, p. 13.

**216 John Lewis residence**
Zermaft, Chester County
1899

*PI*, May 27, 1899, p. 12.

**217 Additions to Episcopal Academy**
Southwest corner of Locust and Juniper Streets,
Philadelphia
1899
Demolished

*PI*, May 27, 1899, p. 12.

**218 Clubhouse for William W. Frazier**
Glenwood Avenue and Old York Road,
Jenkintown
1899
Demolished

*PI*, June 14, 1899, p. 10.

**219 Additions to Warden estate**
Nineteenth Street and Allegheny Avenue,
Philadelphia
1899

*PRERBG*, XIV, no. 39, September 27, 1899.

**220 Alterations to Horace Jayne residence**
320 South Nineteenth Street, Philadelphia
1899

*PI*, October 4, 1899, p. 115.
(cat. 37)

**221 Three-story residence**
States Avenue near Pacific Avenue,
Atlantic City, New Jersey
1899
Demolished

*PI*, October 26, 1899, p. 10.

**222 Additions to Samuel Bettle residence**
Haverford
1899

*PRERBG*, XIV, no. 50, December 13, 1899.

**223 Decorations, Avenue of Fame, G.A.R. Encampment**
Broad Street, Philadelphia
1899
Demolished

*Architectural Annual*, ed. Albert Kelsey,
Philadelphia, 1900, pp. 234–236.

**224 Church of the Atonement**
Forty-seventh Street and Kingsessing Avenue,
Philadelphia
1900

*PI*, January 3, 1900, p. 10.

**225 John C. Bullitt residence, stable and gardener's house**
Paoli
1900

*PI*, January 24, 1900, p. 5.

**226 Arcade Building and pedestrian bridge**
Fifteenth and Market Streets, Philadelphia
1900–1901
Demolished

*PI*, March 21, 1900, p. 9.
(cat. 40)

**227 Rebuilding of 1123 Walnut Street, based on plans made in 1889**
Philadelphia
1900

*PRERBG*, XV, no. 14, April 4, 1900.

**228 Rebuilding of 627 Market Street for the Brierly estate**
Market Street, Philadelphia
1900
Demolished

*PI*, April 18, 1900, p. 11.

**229 8th Ward Settlement House**
Hutchinson and Locust Streets,
Philadelphia
1900
Demolished

*PRERBG*, XV, no. 19, May 9, 1900.

**230 One-story addition to the Second Presbyterian Church**
Twenty-first and Walnut Streets,
Philadelphia
1900

*PI*, July 6, 1900, p. 7.

**231 Chapel of the Prince of Peace Mission of the Holy Trinity Episcopal Church**
Twenty-second and Morris Streets, Philadelphia
1900
Demolished

*PI*, July 6, 1900, p. 7.

**232 Bell tower of the Second Presbyterian Church**
Twenty-first and Walnut Streets,
Philadelphia
1900

*PI*, July 25, 1900, p. 5.

**233 Three-story mill building and one-story warehouse for John T. Lewis and Bros. Company**
Cumberland and Aramingo Streets,
Philadelphia
1900

*PI*, September 1, 1900, p. 13.

**234 Additions to Racquet Club**
923 Walnut Street, Philadelphia
1900
Demolished

*PI*, December 1, 1900, p. 11.

**235 Additions and alterations to 127 South Twelfth Street**
Philadelphia
1900
Demolished

*PI*, December 14, 1900, p. 14.

**236 E. S. Beale residence**
Berwyn
1901

*PRERBG*, XVI, no. 4, January 23, 1901.

**237 Extension of West End Trust Company Building**
Broad Street and South Penn Square,
Philadelphia
1901
Demolished

*PI*, March 28, 1901, p. 15.
(cat. 39)

**238 Additions to Bryn Mawr College**
Bryn Mawr
1901

*PRERBG*, XVI, no. 14, April 3, 1901.

**239 Pennsylvania Railroad Station**
Lansdowne
1901

*PI*, April 5, 1901, p. 9.

**240 Additions to Bryn Mawr Hospital**
Bryn Mawr
1901

*PI*, May 8, 1901, p. 7.

**241 Alterations and additions to DeWitt Cuyler residence**
Haverford
1901
Demolished

*PI*, August 27, 1901, p. 7.

**242 Pennsylvania Railroad Offices**
Filbert Street west of Fifteenth Street,
Philadelphia
1901
Demolished

*PRERBG*, XVI, no. 37, September 11, 1901.

**243 Pennsylvania Railroad Station**
Thirty-second and Market Streets,
Philadelphia
1901–3
Demolished

*PI*, October 11, 1901, p. 11.

**244 H. G. Lloyd stable**
Bryn Mawr
1901–2

*PI*, November 2, 1901, p. 15.

**245 C. W. Middleton stable**
Torresdale, Philadelphia
1901–2

*PI*, November 4, 1901, p. 14.

**246 Pennsylvania Railroad branch of the Y.M.C.A.**
Pitcairn
1902

*PI*, February 1, 1902, p. 11.

**247 Guggenheim Wing, Jewish Hospital**
Broad Street and Old York Road,
Philadelphia
1902
Demolished

*PI*, February 25, 1902, p. 6.
(cat. 4)

**248 Loeb Operating Ward, Jewish Hospital**
Broad Street and Old York Road,
Philadelphia
1902
Demolished

*PI*, March 29, 1902, p. 7.
(cat. 4)

**249 New Grammar School**
Haverford
1902
Altered

*PI*, April 2, 1902, p. 16.

**250 Additions and alterations to William Sellers residence**
1819 Vine Street, Philadelphia
1902
Demolished

*PI*, May 16, 1902, p. 7.

**251 Additions to Provident Bank buildings**
Fourth and Chestnut Streets, Philadelphia
1902
Demolished

*PI*, June 4, 1902, p. 7.
(cat. 14)

**252 Exterior alterations and improvements to Western Savings Fund Society**
Philadelphia
1902
Demolished

*PI*, June 25, 1902, p. 7.

**253 Eisner Home for Nurses, Jewish Hospital**
Broad Street and Old York Road, Philadelphia
1902
Demolished

*PI*, July 14, 1902, p. 13.
(cat. 4)

**254 Alterations to Home for the Aged and Infirm Israelites, Jewish Hospital**
Broad Street and Old York Road,
Philadelphia
1902
Demolished

*PI*, September 3, 1902, p. 11.
(cat. 4)

**255 Pennsylvania Railroad Station**
Edgewood
1902–3

*PI*, September 16, 1902, p. 7.

**256 Double house for Dr. McNichol**
222-224 North Nineteenth Street,
Philadelphia
1902
Demolished

*PI*, January 4, 1902, p. 6.

**257 Buildings for the Home for Consumptives
for the Philadelphia Protestant Episcopal
City Mission**
Stenton Avenue at Evergreen Avenue,
Chestnut Hill, Philadelphia
1903

*PI*, March 27, 1903, p. 4.

**258 Pennsylvania Railroad Station**
Bellewood
1903

*PI*, April 9, 1903, p. 4.

**259 Library addition for H. H. Furness
residence: "Lindenshade"**
Wallingford
1903

*PI*, April 23, 1903, p. 6.

**260 Alterations to Walter Furness residence**
222 West Washington Square, Philadelphia
1903
Demolished

*PI*, May 22, 1903, p. 16.

**261 Pennsylvania Railroad Station**
Port Allegheny
1903

*PI*, June 16, 1903, p. 15.

**262 Alterations to McLentock-Marshall
Construction Company Offices**
Pottstown
1903

*PI*, July 15, 1903, p. 15.

**263 Pennsylvania Railroad Station**
Norristown
1903

*PI*, July 15, 1903, p. 15.

**264 Isolating Ward, Jewish Hospital**
Broad Street and Old York Road,
Philadelphia
1903
Demolished

*PI*, September 19, 1903, p. 15.
(cat. 4)

**265 Three-story restaurant**
Juniper and Sansom Streets,
Philadelphia
1903
Demolished

*PI*, September 5, 1903, p. 9.

**266 House for H. H. Smith**
Cape May, New Jersey
1903

*PI*, November 30, 1903, p. 6.

**267 Alterations to 249-251 West Harvey Street**
Germantown, Philadelphia
1904

*PI*, March 24, 1904, p. 11.

**268 Extensive alterations to the building
formerly owned by the National Bank of the
Republic**
313 Chestnut Street, Philadelphia
1904
Demolished

*PRERBG*, XIX, no. 10, March 9, 1904.
(cat. 25)

**269 Alterations to 125 South Twelfth Street**
Philadelphia
1904
Demolished

*PI*, April 25, 1904, p. 6.

**270 Additions to Arcade Building**
Fifteenth and Market Streets,
Philadelphia
1904
Demolished

*PI*, May 21, 1904, p. 6.
(cat. 40)

**271 Philadelphia Orphans Asylum, near
Wallingford**
Project
Delano and Aldrich won the competition, which
included Cope and Stewardson, Field and
Medary

*PRERBG*, XIX, no. 23, June 8, 1904.

**272 Additions to Home for Consumptives for
the Philadelphia Protestant Episcopal City
Mission**
Stenton Avenue at Evergreen Avenue,
Chestnut Hill, Philadelphia
1904

*PRERBG*, XIX, no. 24, June 15, 1904.

**273 Alterations to H. E. Drayton residence**
2049 Locust Street, Philadelphia
1904

*PRERBG*, XIX, no. 28, July 13, 1904.

**274 George Gerhard, Jr., residence**
Fifty-eighth Street and Overbrook Avenue,
Philadelphia
1904
Demolished

*PRERBG*, XIX, no. 32, August 10, 1904.

**275 Commons Building, Lehigh University**
Bethlehem
1904

*PI*, August 15, 1904, p. 9.

**276 Two residences**
Villanova
1904

*PI*, August 19, 1904, p. 12.

**277 Infirmary for Orphanage**
Sixty-sixth and Lansdowne Streets,
Philadelphia
1904
Demolished

*PI*, September 6, 1904, p. 9.

**278 Pavilion for Church Home**
Fifty-eighth and Baltimore Streets,
Philadelphia
1904

*PI*, September 15, 1904, p. 7.

**279 Standard Ice Manufacturing Plant**
Twenty-fourth and Lombard Streets,
Philadelphia
1904-5
Demolished

*PI*, December 11, 1904, p. 11.

**280 French Street Station, Pennsylvania
Railroad**
Wilmington, Delaware

*PRERBG*, XX, no. 1, January 4, 1905.

**281 Pennsylvania Railroad Station**
East Liberty
1905

*PRERBG*, XX, no. 3, January 18, 1905.

**282 Alterations to the Church of Our Saviour**
Jenkintown
1905

*PI*, March 21, 1905, p. 15.

**283 Two-story laundry, Jewish Hospital**
Broad Street and Old York Road,
Philadelphia
1905
Demolished

*PI*, March 21, 1905, p. 15.
(cat. 4)

**284 Alterations to 125 South Twelfth Street**
Philadelphia
1905
Demolished

*PI*, April 10, 1905, p. 16.

**285 St. Luke's Parish House**
Kensington, Philadelphia
1905

*PI*, April 17, 1905, p. 5.

**286 Remodeling of R. E. Griscom residence**
Haverford
1905

*PI*, May 6, 1905, p. 15.

**287 Remodeling of 218-230 Lombard Street
for the Jewish Sheltering Home**
Philadelphia
1905
Demolished

*PI*, June 8, 1905, p. 11.

**288 Messiah Universalist Home**
York Road and Ruscomb Street,
Philadelphia
1905
Demolished

*PI*, June 14, 1905, p. 9.

**289 Hydro-therapeutic apparatus for the
Guggenheim Wing, Jewish Hospital**
Philadelphia
1905
Demolished

*PI*, June 15, 1905, p. 9.
(cat. 4)

**290 Girard Trust Company**
Broad and Chestnut Streets,
Philadelphia
1905-7
Allen Evans, with McKim, Mead and White

*PI*, March 7, 1905, p. 15.
(fig. 40)

**291 Alterations to Samuel Shipley residence: "Town's End"**
West Chester
1905

Conversation with Mrs. Page Allinson, daughter of Samuel Shipley, July 1972.

**292 Additions to the Merion Cricket Club**
Montgomery Avenue, Haverford
1905

PRERBG, XXI, no. 20, May 16, 1905.
(cat. 34)

**293 Additions to Union League**
1905
Project
Competition lost; other competitors included Price and McLanahan, Cope and Stewardson, Joseph Huston, Edgar Seeler, and Horace Trumbauer

PRERBG, XXI, no. 30, July 26, 1905.

**294 Chapel**
Willow Grove
1905

PI, August 1, 1905, p. 12.

**295 Additions and alterations to the Chapel of the Prince of Peace Mission of Holy Trinity Episcopal Church**
Point Breeze Avenue and Morris Street, Philadelphia
1905
Demolished

PI, December 22, 1905, p. 13.

**296 Garage and stable for Percy Madeira**
Ogontz, Philadelphia
1906
Demolished

PI, February 2, 1906, p. 6.

**297 J. Ogden Hoffman residence**
Villanova
1906

PI, February 6, 1906, p. 5.

**298 Marriott Smith residence**
Wynnewood
1906

PI, February 14, 1906, p. 7.

**299 Alterations to the Church of Our Saviour**
Jenkintown
1906

PI, February 22, 1906, p. 11.

**300 Chapel of the Prince of Peace Mission of Holy Trinity Episcopal Church**
Twenty-second and Morris Streets, Philadelphia
1906
Demolished

PI, March 6, 1906, p. 15.

**301 Wistar Morris stable**
Overbrook
1906

PI, March 16, 1906, p. 11.

**302 Alterations to St. Andrew's Parish House**
Eighth and Spruce Streets, Philadelphia
1906

PI, May 3, 1906, p. 15.

**303 Alterations to 1118 Spruce Street for William Mall**
Philadelphia
1906

PI, June 13, 1906, p. 11.

**304 Drown Memorial Hall, Lehigh University**
Bethlehem
1906

PI, August 3, 1906, p. 6.

**305 Thomas Leaming residence**
Wayne
1906

PI, September 8, 1906, p. 9.

**306 Colonial style residence**
Wayne
1906

PRERBG, XXI, no. 39, September 26, 1906.

**307 Alterations to 242 Chestnut Street for Dr. David Jayne**
Philadelphia
1907
Demolished

PI, March 2, 1907, p. 6.

**308 Three-story building for the Girard Trust Company**
1413–1417 Chestnut Street, Philadelphia
1907
Demolished

PI, March 5, 1907, p. 14.
(fig. 40)

**309 1403 Chestnut Street**
Philadelphia
1907
Demolished

Philadelphia Evening Bulletin, March 25, 1907.

**310 Fire House**
Merion
1907

PRERBG, XXII, no. 5, January 30, 1907.

**311 Alterations to entrance and grounds of Marriott C. Smith residence**
Cherry Lane, Ardmore
1907

PRERBG, XXII, no. 42, October 16, 1907.

**312 Sterilizing room, Jewish Hospital**
Broad Street and Old York Road, Philadelphia
1907
Demolished

PRERBG, XXII, no. 43, October 23, 1907.
(cat. 4)

**313 Additions and alterations to Thomas DeWitt Cuyler residence**
Haverford
1908
Demolished

PRERBG, XXIII, no. 2, January 8, 1908.

**314 Concrete garage for W. F. Stewart**
Haverford
1908

PRERBG, XXIII, no. 8, February 19, 1908.

**315 Additions and alterations to E. B. Cassatt residence**
Berwyn
1908

PI, February 25, 1908, p. 13.

**316 Wilmington Station, Pennsylvania Railroad**
Wilmington, Delaware
1908

PI, June 27, 1908, p. 11.

**317 Additions to Percy Madeira residence**
Ogontz, Philadelphia
1908
Demolished

PI, November 4, 1908, p. 12.

**318 Morris Building**
1400 block, Chestnut Street, Philadelphia
1909–10

Ellis P. Oberholtzer, Philadelphia, a History of the City and Its People, Philadelphia, n.d., IV, p. 78.
(fig. 40)

**319 Additions to Bryn Mawr Hospital**
Bryn Mawr
1910

PRERBG, XXV, no. 1, January 3, 1910.

**320 V. S. Pownell residence**
Swarthmore
1910

PRERBG, XXV, no. 2, January 12, 1910.

**321 T. Zurbrugg residence**
Riverside, New Jersey
1910

PRERBG, XXV, no. 24, June 15, 1910.

**322 Arcade Store Building**
Ardmore
1910

PRERBG, XXV, no. 24, June 15, 1910.

**323 Alterations to Mrs. A. J. Cassatt residence**
Haverford
1910
Demolished

PRERBG, XXV, no. 27, July 6, 1910.

**324 Additions to Charles Harrison residence: "Happy Creek Farm"**
Devon
1910

PRERBG, XXV, no. 28, July 13, 1910.

**325 Odd Fellows Orphanage**
Twentieth Street and Ogontz Avenue, Philadelphia
1911

PRERBG, XXVI, no. 14, April 5, 1911.

**326 M. A. Metz factory**
Sixth Street and Spring Garden, Philadelphia
1911
Demolished

PRERBG, XXVI, no. 11, March 15, 1911.

**327 Additions to Bryn Mawr Hospital**
Bryn Mawr
1911

PRERBG, XXVI, no. 36, September 6, 1911.

Note: Frank Furness died in 1912. The checklist does not include buildings after this date although the firm continued under the name Furness, Evans and Company for another generation.

# Attributed Works

Note: In most instances, the attributions have been initiated on the basis of stylistic evidence. Where direct documentation has not been available, secondary corroborative information has been sought. Family, social, or business connections frequently are to be found; at times, later commissions prove informative. Thus, the houses at the corner of Thirteenth and Irving streets can be safely attributed to Furness on stylistic grounds—the massing is similar to the Frazier house of 1882—and other relationships can be readily discovered. The corner house was owned by John T. Lewis, father-in-law of Allen Evans; the neighboring house by Edward Beale, vice-president of Lewis's paint company. Furness later received commissions for a country house and factory building for Lewis, and a country house for Beale.

Alterations to a pre-existing building provide other important clues. Generally, the architect of the original design is called upon to make alterations. Such was the case when Furness continued the expansion of the Provident buildings, or on a lesser scale, when the firm directed the designs for all of the later additions and alterations to Percy Madeira's residence. The Cassatt residence in Bryn Mawr, which has been attributed to Furness on stylistic grounds, receives additional support in the light of the alteration by Furness in 1910.

Three areas open for further investigation:

1. The 125 or more railroad buildings for the Philadelphia and Reading Railroad: these would undoubtedly include the Mount Airy and Chestnut Hill stations on the Chestnut Hill line, the Wissahickon and Roxborough stations on the Norristown line, and the West Trenton Station, Trenton, New Jersey.
2. Buildings for which Furness, Evans and Company designed additions or alterations after 1890, including the residences of DeWitt Cuyler, A. J. Cassatt, and George Gerhard.
3. Names listed in the Furness sketchbooks, and commissions paid Furness, for which a specific building could be related. These would include: Shober, $300/$500; Harrison, $100; J. Brook, $100; Clark, $125/$700; Gowan, $200; Fraiser, $150; Towne, $125; Bache, $75; E. Brooks, $200; Kingston, $183; DaCosta, $300; Rhodes, $375.

## 328 Thomas McKean residence
1925 Walnut Street, Philadelphia
c. 1869
Demolished
Fraser, Furness and Hewitt

Attribution based on the use of the McKean house as the standard for workmanship in the specifications for the building of the Pennsylvania Academy of the Fine Arts.

## 329 H. Pratt McKean residence
1923 Walnut Street, Philadelphia
c. 1869
Demolished
Fraser, Furness and Hewitt

Attribution based on similarity to the Thomas McKean house at 1925 Walnut Street.

## 330 Franklin Telegraph Company
Third and Chestnut Streets, Philadelphia
c. 1869–70.
Demolished
Fraser, Furness and Hewitt

Attribution by Massey 1, p. 15.

## 331 Henry C. Gibson residence
1612 Walnut Street, Philadelphia
c. 1871
Furness and Hewitt

## 332 T. A. Scott residence
Rittenhouse Square, Philadelphia
c. 1872
Demolished
Furness and Hewitt

Attribution by Massey 2, p. 26.

## 333 2206–2210 Walnut Street
Philadelphia
c. 1873
Part altered, and part demolished.
Furness and Hewitt

Attribution based on drawing in Furness's style showing the entire block and including the John Ashhurst residence; filed under Wilson Eyre in the Historical Society of Pennsylvania (pointed out to us by Edward Teitelman).

## 333A E. C. Evans residence
Haverford
1875
Demolished
Furness and Hewitt

Photograph in Lower Merion Historical Society.

## 334 Store buildings for Francis Fassitt
1207–1209 Market Street, Philadelphia
c. 1876
Frank Furness

Style correlated by family relationship of architect to Fassitt.

## 335 1404–1406 Chestnut Street
Philadelphia
c. 1876
Demolished
Frank Furness

## 336 Insurance Company of North America
232 Walnut Street, Philadelphia
c. 1876
Demolished
Frank Furness

## 337 Block of houses
Spruce and Delancey Streets east of Forty-first Street, Philadelphia
c. 1876
Frank Furness

Property at one time owned by Clarence Clark, whose name appears in several of the Furness sketchbooks, Collection George Wood Furness.

## 338 Ridge Avenue Market
Ridge Avenue below Girard Avenue, Philadelphia
c. 1876
Frank Furness

## 339 Ornamental Stone Gateway
Centennial Exhibition (since moved to East River Drive near Strawberry Mansion Bridge), Philadelphia
1876
Frank Furness

## 340 Horace Howard Furness residence: "Lindenshade"
Wallingford
c. 1878 and later
Demolished except for the library
Frank Furness

Attribution based on the family relationship.

## 341 A. J. Cassatt residence: "Cheswold"
Cheswold Lane, Haverford
c. 1878
Demolished
Frank Furness

## 342 Building (now owned by the Philadelphia Electric Company)
Fortieth Street below Market Street, Philadelphia
c. 1878
Altered
Frank Furness

## 343 Emlen Physic residence
Washington Street, Cape May, New Jersey
1879
Frank Furness

Plans and details are similar to the Rhawn house of the same year.

## 344 2305 and 2305½ St. James Street
Philadelphia
c. 1880
Frank Furness

## 345 Hoopes Brothers and Thomas Nursey
West Chester
c. 1881
To be demolished
Frank Furness

Hoopes Brothers family were in-laws of E. J. Dallet, then a draftsman in Furness's office.

## 346 618 Hazelhurst Avenue
Merion Station
c. 1883
Altered
Furness and Evans

## 347 602 Highland Avenue
Merion Station
c. 1885
Furness and Evans

## 348 610 Hazelhurst Avenue
Merion Station
c. 1885
Altered
Furness and Evans

## 349 John T. Lewis residence
242 South Thirteenth Street, Philadelphia
c. 1885
Altered
Furness and Evans

Lewis was Allen Evans's father-in-law and the client for several other Furness commissions.

## 350 Edward S. Beale residence
240 South Thirteenth Street, Philadelphia
c. 1885
Furness and Evans

Beale was the vice-president of the J. T. Lewis paint factory and the client for other Furness commissions.

**351 124, 126, 128, 130, 132 South Seventeenth Street**
Philadelphia
c. 1885
Three are demolished, two altered
Furness and Evans

**352 Wallingford Station, Pennsylvania Railroad**
Wallingford
c. 1885
Furness and Evans

Family tradition attributes this station to Furness;
cf. Massey 2, p. 28.

**353 Additions to John T. Bailey and Company factory**
Water and Otsego Streets, Philadelphia
c. 1885
Furness and Evans

Later commissions for Bailey make this likely.
(cat. 36)

**354 Carpenter's Lane Station, Pennsylvania Railroad**
Chestnut Hill, Philadelphia
c. 1885
Furness and Evans

The similarity of this design to the Wallingford
Station is striking.

**355 Upsal Station, Pennsylvania Railroad**
Chestnut Hill, Philadelphia
c. 1885
Furness and Evans

The similarity of this design to the Wallingford
Station is striking.

**356 Allen's Lane Station, Pennsylvania Railroad**
Chestnut Hill, Philadelphia
c. 1885
Furness and Evans

The similarity of this design to the Wallingford
Station is striking.

**357 Robert Lewis residence**
123 South Twenty-second Street,
Philadelphia
c. 1886
Furness, Evans and Company

We believe that Lewis was a relative of Allen
Evans.

**358 Horace Howard Furness residence**
Point Pleasant, New Jersey
1886
Furness, Evans and Company

If this commission was actually executed, the
family relationship makes it more than likely
a building by Furness.

**359 Baltimore and Ohio Station**
Newark, Delaware
c. 1886
Furness, Evans and Company

Unsigned drawing in the Historical Society of
Pennsylvania is in the same style as the other,
signed Furness drawings for Baltimore and
Ohio railroad stations.

**360 237–243 South Twenty-first Street**
Philadelphia
c. 1888
Furness, Evans and Company

A later alteration to 2049 Locust Street (243
South Twenty-first Street) in 1904 provides
corroboration.

**361 1320 Locust Street**
Philadelphia
c. 1888
Furness, Evans and Company

Details similar to the Locust Street Development
work, and to the Lewis and Beale houses on
Thirteenth Street.

**362 Alterations to 1023 Market Street**
Philadelphia
c. 1888
Altered
Furness, Evans and Company

Based on similarity of designs to 1025 Market
Street, designed by the firm in 1894.

**363 Firehouse**
313 Branch Street, Philadelphia
c. 1888
Demolished
Furness, Evans and Company

**364 George B. Roberts residence**
Bala
c. 1889
Demolished
Furness, Evans and Company

Business connections make this a likely choice.

**365 Additions to John T. Bailey and Company factory**
Water and Otsego Streets, Philadelphia
1889
Furness, Evans and Company

Based on commission of 1895.
(cat. 36)

**366 J. P. Evans and Company laboratory**
217–219 North Tenth Street, Philadelphia
1893
Furness, Evans and Company
(This building pointed out by D. Stupplebeen.)

## Incorrectly Attributed Works

Note: Frequently, an architect of Furness's
stature is erroneously credited with the designs
of buildings in his style. Several buildings that
have been assigned to Furness are clearly the
work of his contemporaries, including the
following:

**St. Timothy's Workingman's Club**
Ridge Avenue, Wissahickon,
Philadelphia
c. 1873
Charles M. Burns

Cf. Campbell Collection, Historical Society of
Pennsylvania.

**Joseph Potts residence**
3905 Spruce Street, Philadelphia
c. 1876
Wilson Brothers

Wilson Brothers, A Catalogue of the Work,
Philadelphia, 1885, p. 7.

**Wayne Station, Pennsylvania Railroad**
Wayne
1881
Wilson Brothers

Wilson Brothers, A Catalogue of the Work,
Philadelphia, 1885, p. 12.

**McDaniel Mausoleum, Woodlands Cemetery**
Fortieth Street and Woodlawn Avenue,
Philadelphia
c. 1875
Signed: H. Q. French, New York

**St. Stephen's Parish House**
Tenth Street below Market Street,
Philadelphia
1888
George C. Mason

Minutes of the congregation of St. Stephen's
parish.

**Central National Bank**
Wilmington, Delaware
c. 1890
Baker and Dallett

Philadelphia and Popular Philadelphians,
Philadelphia, 1891, p. 222.

**Crescent Boat Club**
East River Drive, Philadelphia
c. 1890
Charles Balderston

PI, March 9, 1891, p. 7.

**Girard Trust Company (later Colonial Trust Company)**
2020 Chestnut Street, Philadelphia
1878
Demolished
George Hewitt

Philadelphia and Popular Philadelphians,
Philadelphia, 1891, p. 223.

**Devon Station, Pennsylvania Railroad**
Devon
c. 1884
G. W. and W. D. Hewitt

AABN, XV, January 12, 1884, p. 25.

# Addendum to the Checklist

George E. Thomas, Hyman Myers,
and Jeffrey A. Cohen

In the fourteen years that have elapsed since the checklist of works was published significant new commissions have been discovered that considerably enlarge our understanding of Frank Furness's career. Other projects that were known have proven to be of greater significance after further investigation, and would probably have warranted inclusion in the illustrated catalogue. Such is the case with the Latta Crabtree cottage in the New Jersey resort of Lake Hopatcong, and with the spectacular renovations to the New York City house of Theodore Roosevelt, Sr., executed in the 1870s, which introduced Furness to Roosevelt's son, the future president, and eventually to the American west. Perhaps of greatest interest is the cluster of designs at Bar Harbor in Maine, discovered by Earle Shettleworth, Jr., of the Maine Historic Preservation Commission, and published with an essay by James F. O'Gorman in *A Biographical Dictionary of Architects in Maine,* vol. 2, no. 9, June 1985. Many of these commissions were supervised by William Masters Camac, who summered in Bar Harbor, indicating that he, like L.C. Baker and E.J. Dallett, had independent commissions within the Furness office. In addition, a considerable amount of new information has come to light about Furness as a furniture designer, which has been the subject of scholarship by Wendy Kaplan for the Museum of Fine Arts in Boston, and by David A. Hanks for the Philadelphia Museum of Art. See, in particular, Kaplan, "The furniture of Frank Furness," *The Magazine Antiques,* vol. 131, no. 5 (May 1987), pp. 1088–95; Hanks and Page Talbott, "Daniel Pabst—Philadelphia Cabinetmaker," *Bulletin: Philadelphia Museum of Art,* vol. 73, no. 316 (April 1977), pp. 1–24; and also Metropolitan Museum of Art, *In Pursuit of Beauty: Americans and the Aesthetic Movement* (New York, 1986), pp. 145–47, 174, 430–31. A related commission, discovered in a collection of newspaper clippings assembled by historian Thompson Westcott (see no. 377), was for a six by eight foot "banner or shield, exhibiting a variety of native American woods," designed by Furness for William H. Lippincott and displayed at the Paris Universal Exposition of 1878.

In the previous checklist some commissions were overlooked; others were either listed in error, such as the Roxborough Baptist Church, actually designed by Isaac Hobbs, or were inaccurately noted in the original documents and therefore mislocated, such as the Church of St. Michael's at 42nd and Wallace streets, which was, in fact, constructed and still stands a block to the west at 43rd and Wallace streets. Since the checklist was first published, *The Biographical Dictionary of Philadelphia Architects, 1700–1930* (Boston, 1985), assembled by Sandra Tatman and Roger Moss, has added another half-dozen commissions; they have been gracious enough to allow us to consult their documentation for these on file at the Athenaeum of Philadelphia. Finally, we are indebted to Jeffrey A. Cohen's new scholarship and are pleased to acknowledge his contribution by listing him as co-author of this revision.

May 1987                                                                                    G.E.T./H.M.

## Additions

**367 Competition for the Masonic Temple of Philadelphia**
1867
Project
Competition lost to James H. Windrim

Diary of Henry Augustus Sims, September 16, 1867, in Leslie Beller, "The Diary of Henry Augustus Sims," M.A. Thesis, University of Pennsylvania, 1976, p. 39.

**368 Redesign of the Philadelphia and Reading Railroad Terminal**
Broad and Callowhill Streets, Philadelphia
1867
Unexecuted

George E. Thomas, "Design for the Philadelphia and Reading Railroad, Broad Street Depot," in James F. O'Gorman, Jeffrey A. Cohen, George E. Thomas, and G. Holmes Perkins, *Drawing Toward Building: Philadelphia Architectural Graphics, 1732–1986* (Philadelphia, 1986), pp. 128–29.

**369 Competition for the Philadelphia Saving Fund Society Building**
Seventh and Walnut Streets, Philadelphia
1868
Project
Competition lost to Addison Hutton

Elizabeth B. Yarnall, *Addison Hutton, Quaker Architect, 1834–1916* (Philadelphia, 1974), p. 42.

**370 (see no. 328) H. Pratt McKean residence**
1923 Walnut Street, Philadelphia
1869
Demolished

Letter from Miller McKim to Charles F. McKim, September 21, 1869, in the Library of Congress, Washington, D.C.

**371 (see no. 329) Thomas McKean residence**
1925 Walnut Street, Philadelpha
1869
Demolished

Ibid.

**372 Second National Bank**
Franklin and Market Streets, Wilkes-Barre
1870
Altered

Identified as the work of John Fraser in a newspaper clipping transcribed c. 1940 by Edward Phillips in his unpublished typescript "History of Wilkes-Barre and Luzerne County," volume titled "Miscellany," Wyoming Historical and Geological Society, Wilkes-Barre. The date suggests that this was the work of Fraser, Furness, and Hewitt (pointed out to us by Michael J. Lewis).

**373 Northern Savings Fund Society**
Sixth and Spring Garden Streets, Philadelphia
1871

*Public Ledger,* July 18, 1872, p. 4.

**374 Unidentified house**
c. 1874

Signed linens in the Athenaeum of Philadelphia.

**375 "Castle Ringstetten" of Undine Barge Club**
Kelly Drive at Falls of Schuylkill, Philadelphia
1875

Specifications dated October 22, 1875, at Undine Barge Club.

**376 Renovations to Theodore Roosevelt, Sr., residence**
6 West Fifty-seventh Street, New York, New York
c. 1875

Drawings in the Furness sketchbooks, Collection George Wood Furness, and Roosevelt family correspondence.

**377 (see no. 342) West Philadelphia Institute**
Fortieth and Ludlow Streets, Philadelphia
1876
Altered

Thompson Westcott, comp., "Scrap Book, Buildings, Public Places, Public Things," 3 vols. (c. 1874–80), vol. 1, p. 28, in the Historical Society of Pennsylvania.
(correction of no. 40)

**378 Maternity Ward, Women's Hospital of Philadelphia**
Twenty-second Street and North College Avenue, Philadelphia
1877
Demolished

*18th Annual Report of the Board of Managers,* January 1879, pp. 5–6.
(distinct from no. 35?)

**379 (see no. 337) Development on Spruce and Irving Streets, West Philadelphia**
Probably 4047–61 Spruce Street and 4050–66 Irving Street, Philadelphia
c. 1877

Westcott scrapbooks, vol. 1, p. 102, in the Historical Society of Pennsylvania.

**380 Alterations and two-story addition to Reform Club for Ladies**
1520 Chestnut Street, Philadelphia
c. 1878

Westcott scrapbooks, vol. 1, p. 164, in the Historical Society of Pennsylvania.

**381 Harrison Earl residence: "Earlham"**
Unspecified location in Philadelphia suburbs
c. 1880

Wells and Hope, comp., *Philadelphia Suburban Homes Part I* (Philadelphia, c. 1889), in the Historical Society of Pennsylvania.

**382 (see no. 332) Thomas A. Scott residence**
Nineteenth Street and South Rittenhouse Square, Philadelphia
c. 1880?
Demolished

*Harper's Weekly,* vol. 34, no. 1738 (April 12, 1890), p. 270.

**383 Watchman's Boxes for the Pennsylvania Railroad**
1882

Drawings in the Architectural Archives, Fine Arts Library, University of Pennsylvania.

**384 Passenger station for the Perkiomen branch of the Pennsylvania Railroad**
Collegeville
1884
Demolished

Drawings in the Architectural Archives, Fine Arts Library, University of Pennsylvania.

**385 (see no. 91) Three or four cottages near Breslin Hotel**
Lake Hopatcong, New Jersey
1885

*Building* (New York), vol. 3, no. 14 (October 1885), p. 156.

**386 Central National Bank**
Wilmington, Delaware
1885

Listed as the work of Baker and Dallett while they were in the office of Furness and Evans, *Philadelphia and Popular Philadelphians* (Philadelphia, 1891), p. 222.
(correction of incorrectly reattributed work, see p. 211)

**387 Classroom and auditorium building for Haverford College**
1885
Project
Unexecuted

Signed drawing dated May 25, 1885, at Haverford College Library.

**388 Summer house for George Preston**
Cazenovia, New York
1885

*Cazenovia Republican* (New York), August 13, 1885.

**389 Wooten wing of Reading Hospital**
Reading
1886
Demolished

*The Reading Journal,* June 5, 1886.

**390 Alterations to and decorative painting of St. Michael's Protestant Episcopal Church**
Birdsboro
1886

Daniel K. Miller, *The History of St. Michael's Protestant Episcopal Church, Birdsboro, Pennsylvania, 1851–1951* (Birdsboro, 1951), p. 33.

**391 Summer cottage for H.C. Hart**
Bar Harbor, Maine
1886
William Masters Camac in charge

James F. O'Gorman, "Frank Furness," in Earle Shettleworth, ed., *A Biographical Dictionary of Architects in Maine,* vol. 2, no. 9, June 1985.

**392 Commercial building for Dr. Rogers**
Bar Harbor, Maine
1886–87
William Masters Camac in charge

Ibid.

**393 Commercial building for Dunbar Brothers**
Bar Harbor, Maine
1886–87
William Masters Camac in charge

Ibid.

**394 William A. Patton residence**
Radnor
1887

*PRERBG,* II, no. 18, May 9, 1887.

**395 Two residences for Francis I. Gowen**
Mount Airy, Philadelphia
1888

*PRERBG,* III, no. 26, July 2, 1888.

**396 Additions and alterations to Alexander Cassatt residence**
220 South Nineteenth Street, Philadelphia
1888
Demolished

Drawings in the Historical Society of Pennsylvania.

**397 Sixth Pennsylvania Lancers' battle monument**
Gettysburg
1888
Frank Furness in charge

*Report of the Pennsylvania Monument Commission,* vol. 2, 1904, p. 835.

**398 Charles Chauncey residence**
Elm Station
1889

*PRERBG,* IV, no. 23, June 12, 1889.

**399 New Castle Public Library**
New Castle, Delaware
1890

*PRERBG,* V, no. 29, July 23, 1890.

**400 Sailors' Home**
Swanson and Catharine Streets, Philadelphia
1890

*PRERBG,* V, no. 27, July 9, 1890.

**401 First National Bank of Montrose**
Montrose
c. 1890
Demolished
Allen Evans in charge

Brochure, Peerless Brick Company, c. 1890.

**402 General Grubb residence**
Beverly, New Jersey
c. 1890

Ibid.

**403 Church of Our Father, Protestant Episcopal chapel**
Hull's Cove, Mount Desert, Maine
1890–91
William Masters Camac in charge

O'Gorman, "Furness."

**404 Alterations to the ferryboat *Chicago* for the Pennsylvania Railroad**
1891

Linens dated July 1891, private collection.

**405 Interior remodeling to the ferryboat *Princeton* for the Pennsylvania Railroad**
c. 1895

Undated linens, private collection.

**406 Interior designs for the ferryboat *New Jersey* for the Pennsylvania Railroad**
1895

Linens dated August 19, 1895, in George E. Thomas, "The Ferryboat New Jersey," in O'Gorman, Cohen, Thomas, and Perkins, *Drawing Toward Building,* p. 172.

**407 Cottage for Professor W.W. Frazier**
Northeast Harbor, Mount Desert, Maine
1895
William Masters Camac in charge

O'Gorman, "Furness."

**408 Interior designs for the ferryboat *New Brunswick* for the Pennsylvania Railroad**
1897

Linens dated 1897, private collection.

**409 Cottage for Henry R. Hatfield: "Thingvilla"**
Kebo Road, Bar Harbor, Maine
1900–1901

O'Gorman, "Furness."

**410 Ferryboat *Baltimore* for the Pennsylvania Railroad**
1901

Linens dated May 1901, private collection.

**411 Interior designs for the ferryboat *Jersey City* for the Pennsylvania Railroad**
1901

Linens dated 1901, private collection.

**412 Alterations to Black Rock Farm**
Gladwynne
c. 1905

Mabel T. Priestman, *Artistic Houses* (Chicago, 1910), pp. 65–72.

**413 Marion H. Smyth residence**
Wynnewood
1906

*PRERBG,* XXI, no. 6, February 7, 1906.

**414 College Commons (Lamberton Hall), Lehigh University**
Bethlehem
1906

Blueprint of signed basement plan in the Athenaeum of Philadelphia.

**415 Additions and alterations to the Philadelphia National Bank**
421 Chestnut Street, Philadelphia
1908

Signed drawings in the Athenaeum of Philadelphia.

**416 Alterations to the Philadelphia Suburban Gas and Electric Company**
700 Locust Street, Philadelphia
1901
Altered

Signed drawings in the Athenaeum of Philadelphia.

## Deletions

Note: A number of additions to the list of attributions can be made based principally on style, but also on some secondary documentation. One of the most important groups consists of buildings photographed for the files of Reading contractor Levi Focht, builder of the Wooten wing of Reading Hospital (see no. 389), and of most, if not all, of the Philadelphia and Reading Railroad structures that Furness referred to in his letter to John E. Wooten of December 23, 1884 (see no. 84). These photographs show numerous houses that Focht built, including the Perkins residence in Bryn Mawr, probably from Furness's designs. Also noteworthy in this collection, and probably also by Furness, is a large country house for Curtin Winsor near Winsor Lane in Haverford, c. 1883 (of which only the barn, since converted into a residence, now survives).

Similarly conjectural is the attribution of the J. Dundas Lippincott residence at 507 South Broad Street, built in 1882, according to a note in the *AABN* (June 17, 1882) and the date on a downspout. Shortly after their departure from Furness, Evans and Company to form their own firm in December 1888, Louis C. Baker and E. James Dallett would list Lippincott as a reference to their abilities in *Illustrated Philadelphia: Its Wealth and Industries* (New York, 1889), p. 174. Along with the strong personalization of the Queen Anne here and the strong Princeton affiliations of Baker and both Lippincott and his wife, this reference hints that it might have been a commission entrusted to Baker while he was working in the firm of Furness and Evans (see no. 386 for a similar situation).

Finally, although we have attempted to restrain ourselves in this category, the rarity of documented interiors by Furness leads us to include the following attribution based on stylistic characteristics but without any kind of documentary support yet revealed: the interior of an unknown house depicted in a photograph (c. 1880) in the collection of the Society for the Preservation of New England Antiquities in Boston. The photograph, published in Peter Thornton, *Authentic Decor: The Domestic Interior, 1620–1920* (London, 1984), p. 340, was taken by J.A. Williams of Newport, Rhode Island, suggesting the house's location as Newport, where Furness had worked as early as the 1870s (see no. 15).

**9 St. James Episcopal Church**
This was actually designed by Emlen Littell, who was connected to a prominent Episcopal family, and who established a career for himself in New York. (Leslie L. Beller, "The Diary of Henry Augustus Sims," M.A. Thesis, University of Pennsylvania, 1976, p. 9.)

**40 West Philadelphia Hall**
Corrected as **West Philadelphia Institute** (see no. 377).

**43 Roxborough Baptist Church**
Church records indicate that Isaac Hobbs, whose designs appeared for many years in *Godey's Lady's Book,* was the architect.

**335 1404–1406 Chestnut Street**
Credited as the work of P. Roney Williamson in *AABN,* II, September 15, 1877, plate.

**338 Ridge Avenue Market**
Documents in the Supplee family indicate that this was the work of Davis E. Supplee (active 1870–1900).

**352 Wallingford station, Pennsylvania Railroad**
A more likely attribution for this is to the office of William Brown, architect for the Pennsylvania Railroad in the 1880s and 1890s.